THE JOSIAH GENERATION

OLLY GOLDENBERG

RIVER
PUBLISHING

THE
JOSIAH
GENERATION

NEW DAWN, NEW RULES, NEW RULERS

ollygoldenberg
FOREWORD BY COLIN DYE

River Publishing & Media Ltd
Barham Court
Teston
Maidstone
Kent
ME18 5BZ
United Kingdom

info@river-publishing.co.uk

All Scripture quotations are taken from the New King James Version (NKJV) © 1982 by Thomas Nelson, Inc.

ISBN 978-1-908393-02-9

Printed in the United Kingdom

Contents

Dedication

Dedicated to the Josiah Generation.
May you run the race to the end!

Acknowledgements

There are many people without whom this book would not have been possible – both in the practical writing of it and for their part in the journey so far.

Thanks to my parents who gave me a godly foundation and have always been a source of support and encouragement at every stage of my life.

Thanks to Tim Pettingale and Jonathan Bugden for all your wisdom, support, friendship and invaluable advice along the way.

Special thanks to Colin and Amanda Dye for your love and support during our years of ministry at Kensington Temple. Thanks to the whole family at KT, you will always be our home. Thank you to the children and young people who, through their desire to serve God, provided many of the testimonies in this book; to the amazing leaders who followed the vision and leadership to see God do great things in the next generation; and to our core team at KT, who never stopped loving us and remain our close friends.

Thanks to Mark Melluish and all at St Paul's Ealing – thank you for adopting us into your family with open arms and standing with us as we step out.

Finally, thanks to my family: my four gorgeous boys who God has blessed me with – it is a real joy to watch you grow with the Lord; to my darling wife who has stood by me, read and re-read the manuscript, affirmed me in my call and loved me beyond anything I could have imagined – thank you for being the woman I needed in each season.

What Others Are Saying About This Book...

"Olly Goldenberg is not a theorist with a good idea. He is a seasoned practitioner who has honed his skills on the frontline of children's ministry for over two decades.

As a result he speaks into the arena of children's ministry with an authority that few can match. It is always exciting to hear of children's lives being transformed by the power of Jesus, but this book gives us more than that – this is the story of Jesus working through children to transform the lives of others.

It is inspirational and transformational, but at the same time very accessible."

John Coles
Director, New Wine

"This book will not just shake you, it will totally transform your heart. Olly speaks with theological understanding and with experience that has seen this lived out.

Whether you are a senior leader in the church, a youth or children's minister, a parent or someone who is wondering what God is up to with this emerging generation – this book is for you.

Read it carefully, its fire is catching."

Daphne Kirk
Generation 2 generation

"This is a word for this generation. A challenge for them to enter into their inheritance as prophetic people.

The call is to hear the voice of God and speak His life-changing words to others."

Barry Kissell
Associate Rector, St Mary's Bryanston Square

"What a wonderful, informative book from a proven leader! You will be equipped and inspired as you read the real life stories of children who know who they are in Christ.

Olly's insights into the life of the young king Josiah clearly help us to know the task at hand: recognising and releasing children to make a difference in this world – NOW!

I highly recommend that you pick up The Josiah Generation and start reading today."

Cathie Clancy
Overflow Kids

"This book is full of stunning stories of children embracing the kingdom of God because it truthfully does belong to them. Olly raises the bar here for us all to see children as God sees them!

This study on the life of young Josiah is a must read for all church leaders, parents and would-be equippers of a generation of world-changers."

Andy Kennedy
King's Kids England, a ministry of YWAM

"Hope is alive and well!

There is a generation arising who will see entire cities saved and nations transformed for the glory of God. In his book, *The Josiah Generation*, Olly Goldenberg boldly declares not only what God intends to do in a generation, but what He is currently doing.

Olly calls us to pour ourselves out for a generation who were born to do great things for God and shine brilliantly in the midst of darkness. Olly's message is both challenging and encouraging as he takes us on a journey full of wisdom, clarity, and revelation.

As I read the testimonies coming out from his ministry, faith began to surge within me, calling me to believe for a generation who are leaders now, who have fully embraced that nothing is impossible with God.

I am grateful for leaders like Olly Goldenberg who are pouring themselves out for a generation and, at the same time, challenging us to do the same. This book will not only train you, but even more importantly than that, it will impart to you the courage necessary to see revival."

Banning Liebscher
Jesus Culture Director

"This book is easy to read, insightful about children's ministry and packed full of stories and wisdom. I would encourage every pastor, children's ministry leader and parent to buy it and be envisioned about what a generation might do if we encourage them."

Mark Melluish
Regional Director, New Wine London and South East

Foreword

The times we live in hang in the balance. As we've seen recently, nations can be turned upside down in an instant. Be it through the uprising of people groups, economic instability, natural disasters or the rise of alternative religions, there is a great shaking happening throughout the world and those things we thought to be eternally solid evaporate quickly. The question is, who will carry the gospel of Jesus Christ to turn the nations back to God? It's time for a generation to arise who know their God and carry His message to the ends of the earth.

I firmly believe we do not live in the time of the super ministers, but rather the age of the saints! That is, a time when the saints, the people of God, begin to arise in the power God and proclaim the gospel with signs and wonders! At Kensington Temple London City Church we have been busy over the last ten years working with a cell model of church. Each member is learning to take their place in a small group setting where they are trained and equipped to be a person of power, seasoning every level of society with the Good News. Over the last ten years we have trained over 10,000 people to the level of cell leadership and then released them throughout London and the whole of the world!

Shortly into our transition into cell church, we began to realise that it is never too early to begin training young people in the ways of the Lord. As we undertook training the youngest, we saw even babies worshipping and bringing the glory of God down. In fact, the children proved to be amongst the most fruitful cell leaders, with as many as 30 other children under their care and in their cells.

All of this work progressed under my direction through the ministry of Oliver Goldenberg and his wife Helen. In this book, Olly has laid out clearly the vision which has burned in his heart during his fifteen years as children's pastor at Kensington Temple. I first met Olly in 1995 as he was completing his training as a medical doctor. Shortly after that the Lord called him to full time ministry and I gave him the full time position of Children's Pastor - a much needed function in the church. I saw that God had given him a revelation that esteems each child to live to their full potential - the call that is on their lives as the Josiah Generation. Never despise the children. Do not make the mistake of underestimating little ones as "cute", and then wait for them to become adults so you can equip them. The Bible gives us sound wisdom to *"train up a child in the way he should go, and when he is old he will not depart from it"* (Proverbs 22:6).

This groundbreaking book is filled with stories that will challenge you and your faith to the core. Children as young as five winning their friends to the Lord, flowing in words of knowledge, seeing their families turned around, seeing healing through prayer, and bringing the glory of God into their environments! Children are leading groups as large as some churches here in England. It is all supernaturally natural and part of the necessary shift where the people of God begin to display His power in everyday life.

As Olly and his family begin to take steps beyond Kensington Temple with my blessing, I want to challenge you prophetically concerning the message he brings. That is, to recognise that a new generation is in your midst. This Josiah generation has the potential to reform their nation for God. You have a key part to play as you recognise and release that potential, instead of leaving the children to fall prey to the world and the enemy. My prayer is that you will stand in the blessing of raising this generation to be gospel carriers and take up their mantle to usher in the kingdom of God in this land.

Colin Dye,
London, June 2011

1
A New Generation

The day I became redundant

The girl who sat next to me was nine years old and had just given her life to Jesus. It was her first time in a church building and her parents knew nothing of God. In fact, her only contact with the church was through a friend in her class who had been telling her about Jesus and had invited her along that day. Now we were chatting together after the meeting.

Being with a baby believer is always a special moment. There is that sense of new life. It's like when you hold a new baby in your arms. For those first few minutes of life you know that you have not only witnessed a miracle, but also that you are holding something fragile, infinitely precious and, at this moment in time, a blank canvas. I get that same feeling when talking with a new believer on the night they are saved. Each time I feel the possibilities that are held in my arms and the responsibility on my shoulders to nurture that young destiny.

So this was my opportunity to add something to this baby believer's life. With the kind of smile reserved for the newborn, I shared with her how she could talk with Jesus any time, any place.

"Oh, I know, my friend already told me ... and I've been reading the Bible she gave me," she said.

I was beginning to sense that I was not really needed here – her friend seemed to have done so much of the preparatory work. But as the children's pastor of the church, I saw it as my role to encourage every child to move on one step more with God.

"You know you can join one of our small groups," I told her, still smiling.

"I already go to the group my friend runs in school each week."

I had one more thing I wanted her to know about: our special weekends away where children could encounter God called, simply, *Encounters.*

"We run weekends away for children to meet with God."

"My friend told me all about the Encounters; I would love to come on one."

There was nothing more for me to add, nothing for me to do. Who was this young leader who had so prepared her friend? She had led her friend into salvation and discipled her beyond anything she had been trained to do, certainly beyond the norm for church as we know it today. At the age of nine she had demonstrated her call as a member of the *Josiah Generation.*

She is not alone.

There is a whole generation of children and young people who God has been preparing to assault the earth in response to His call.

Individual leaders need a generation

Throughout history God has always raised up individuals to reveal Himself to the world and, at strategic times, He has raised up whole generations to fulfil His purposes.

History teaches us that often, when individuals are raised up by

God, they influence other people only during the period of time in which they are active. For example, in the time of the Judges, God raised up successive individual leaders who the people followed for a time. But when the Judge was no longer present to influence them, the people quickly returned to doing whatever they wanted. Without the leadership of a Judge, the whole generation would relapse.

It is God's method to work through anointed leaders. But from time to time, He not only raises up individual leaders – He causes many others to be raised up around them who share their vision and call. In other words, He raises up a whole generation who are "on the same page". Those who are called to be leaders respond to God, but many others also hear and respond. When God brings about such seasons, the leaders need the people as much as the people need their leaders and they move together as one to fulfil God's mandate.

When a whole generation rises up, great things can happen – real, dynamic change in both the spiritual and the natural landscape can take place.

Joshua is an example of a man who led a generation that was prepared for battle. The previous generation, under Moses, had been unwilling to fulfil their mandate and enter the Promised Land. But Joshua's generation rolled up their sleeves and got on with the job at hand. Many have recognised and referred to the contemporary "Joshua generation" – those in their twenties and early thirties who are called of God to break into new territories. But God's plans are continuing as He prepares a spiritual generation that is following after them: *the Josiah Generation*.

King David is recognised as one of the greatest kings ever, but David's army was so effective that often, he was not even needed for them to win battles. Some of his crack troops were so powerful that they became known as David's mighty men. Without these men David would not have been so mighty himself and the nation of Israel would not have expanded its territory in the way that it did. Despite David's obvious anointing, he needed a whole generation to rise up with him to fulfil their destiny, sharing in his God-given mission. He needed to reproduce his anointing and call in others.

Every parent has DNA that they share with their children. It's what makes children inherit their parents' characteristics. Similarly, great leaders demonstrate their greatness by passing on their spiritual DNA to those around them. Their influence means that those who are following them inherit their characteristics. This is how, as the DNA continues to replicate, a whole generation can be influenced.

This is not something that can be manufactured – it is simply a move of God. God is ultimately the one who decides what DNA is passed on. The rising of a new generation does not happen by some slick marketing campaign or by throwing loads of money at our churches' children's programmes. Nor is it something that happens quickly, contrary to our modern desires. Nowadays, if we have to wait one minute for something to download from the Internet this tests our patience! No, when it comes to God's kingdom there are no shortcuts to making disciples, no bargain basement offers. It requires God to move and work in the lives of individuals as they take up the cost of following Him.

As God works simultaneously in the lives of lots of different individuals, He prepares a much larger but complete picture. Like assembling a jigsaw puzzle, people are divinely placed and positioned, then linked with those around them in a widespread, seamless network. This is how God prepares a whole generation to be raised up. Every person God calls must take their place to fulfil His mandate.

Right now God is at work raising up the Josiah Generation to continue His work.

So what does this Josiah Generation look like? In subsequent chapters we will explore its many facets, but for now let's note two important characteristics: this move of God will be noted for its hands-on involvement of ordinary believers and for its radical approach to kingdom ministry.

In the hands of the ordinary believer

In the days of the early church there were apostles who moved under the anointing of the Holy Spirit and were involved in founding and leading the church, but there were also ordinary, everyday believers who served God with a simplicity of heart.

When the early church was persecuted it was the ordinary believers who were scattered initially, while the apostles remained in Jerusalem. As these believers went from place to place they gossiped the gospel. They had been equipped to live for God wherever they went. They were a generation who were prepared to fulfil their destiny.

In modern Christianity we are seeing an increasing shift away from "superstar" ministries to the action of ordinary believers on the street, simply living for God. God is not raising up a few, highly anointed key leaders to do all the work. Instead, He is raising up a whole generation of individuals to bring about change.

Ryan is one such individual.

One day Ryan and John were in their school toilets when a bully came in and slapped Ryan around the face for no reason. John wanted to hit the bully back, but Ryan looked at the bully with the compassion of God and lovingly said,

"You know, you have a real problem."

Then he simply walked away.

A week later the bully came up to him. For a whole week this issue had been eating away inside him; his conscience was stirred and held him ransom. Finally, he had no choice. Contrary to the unwritten code of an inner city teenager, he had to say sorry. Ryan was quick to accept his apology and went on to lead him to the Lord. From then on, Ryan met with him every week in school to help him grow with God.

Ryan is a part of the *Josiah Generation*.

Radical Generation

Some people will feel threatened by this generation because of their radical nature, for there will be many radical elements to them. But in truth they can be considered *radically normal!* This will be a radical change from the norm we are used to, but more importantly, it will be a radical return to the norm that God has set.

The Josiah Generation radicals are the ones who simply get on with the job at hand and do what they are told to do. They are merely reverting to the normal "template" that God intended from the beginning, modelled by the early church believers. These are people whose lives are not held ransom to traditions and methods that can hinder the advance of God's kingdom.

The younger generation is often perceived to be more rebellious, more at risk, and more vulnerable than the older generation were when they were young. In truth, they are often just misunderstood. If we can understand what God is doing through them and allow them to have bold visions, then God's kingdom will advance more rapidly.

The Josiah Generation is so radical that if the previous generations of church are not prepared, they will find it difficult or even impossible to cope with them. As a result they could miss the move that God is bringing through this younger generation. This is a mistake that has been seen in history many times before...

One young generation, seeking to modernise the worship in church, was labelled by some as "agents of the devil" and the instruments they brought in, "instruments of evil". Many have echoed the sentiments of John Wesley, the Methodist leader, when he said, "I have no objections to instruments of music in our chapels, provided they are neither heard nor seen."

The introduction of the organ in some churches was seen as a controversial act!

General Booth, founder of the Salvation Army, took the popular secular tunes of his day and gave them Christian lyrics in order to help reach the unreached. Not all sectors of the church understood what he was doing.

Very often, mature believers find themselves trapped in a limited understanding of who God is and how He operates. For them, God has lost His unpredictability.

Such an entrenched mindset is the type of thing that caused some believers in Wales to spend the entirety of the Welsh revival praying for revival, not realising that they were already living in it! They missed the very revival they had spent decades praying for.

This is why every new generation needs to be allowed the space to not only express its spirituality before God, but to fulfil its mandate from Him unobstructed by others.

Yes, they will need the wise counsel of those who have gone before them to ensure they don't deviate from the Word of God, but that counsel has to be given in the context of understanding their unique destiny.

In my old school there were a set of temporary buildings that had been put in place immediately after the Second World War. People referred to them as "the tin huts". Painted bright green, they stood out like a sore thumb amidst the period buildings that surrounded them.

When they were first built the country was in a deep crisis, so the temporary nature of their construction was no surprise. The surprise was that they still stood and were in use over forty years later!

Eventually, some smart alec discovered the poisonous asbestos in them and only then were they torn down and replaced with something in keeping with the character of the other school buildings.

As we pass on the baton of faith to the next generation we have a responsibility to ensure that they have the freedom to knock down the temporary structures that may have become dear to us, because God will give them insight to see things that are hidden from our eyes.

This generation will offend traditions that we hold dear, but this is a healthy process. Unless our traditions are challenged from time to time, we don't realise what they mean to us, let alone the fact that we have often allowed them to become obstructive to God's plans. Some aspects of church tradition have become so embedded in our thinking that we wrongly think of them as coming from God Himself.

In the short term, the resulting change will be unsettling for those who are accustomed to and happy with church as they know it. But in the long term, something that is more in character with church as God intended will result.

While each new move of God seeks to correct the flaws it sees in previous movements of God's kingdom, many often end up repeating the same mistakes, simply in a different format. Others movements create their own mistakes. But no move of God takes place without some disruption, shaking and unsettlement.

We could spend hours criticising each other for all that we think the other is doing wrong, but all we really need to see is a restoratoin of God's standards for His church.

As persecution increases in the church, so there is a need for a greater purity in understanding and a closer following of God's Word. The darker the days, the brighter the church's light will shine, but this in turn requires a greater degree of courage and boldness among individual believers so that they are able to stand.

Many people are sensing these imminent changes that God is bringing to His church. They see the gap between church as God intended and church as it is today. They know things need to change, but they are not always sure what needs to change, let alone how to bring it about. *The Josiah Generation will be the ones to change it.*

The Josiah Generation

It takes a radical generation to be able to move God's church forward. Many have prophesied over the preceding generation that they are called to be the *Joshua Generation*. And indeed, many in their twenties and early thirties are starting to break into the land and take on new territory. But God's work does not stop there. Now the *Josiah Generation* is needed to take things to the next level.

This new generation that is being raised up by God is so called because it is modelled on the life of the great king, Josiah. In the following chapters, as we study different elements of Josiah's life, we will look at how many of the principles that can be learned from him are being outworked in the generation of children that God is now raising up. A great responsibility hangs on them concerning the fate of many and, as such, a great responsibility falls on us to understand their call and help lead them into it. But in order to prepare them to respond to their call, *we first need to understand that call ourselves*. I pray that this book will be a step in that direction for many.

The Joshua Generation takes new territories, but the Josiah Generation brings a wave of restoration that transforms the very landscape of society, not simply in one area but across national and denominational boundaries.

God is raising up a culture-changing generation who will bring restoration across all levels of society, breaking through boundaries that have been established for generations.

The Josiah Generation has been born!

2

Born Into Royalty

"[King Ammon] *was buried in his tomb in the garden of Uzza. Then Josiah his son reigned in his place.*"
(2 Kings 21:26)

My dad's the king

Alex was a part of our church. He was seven years old and had been coming ever since he was born. He loved Jesus and loved telling people about Jesus. One day in school, Alex was speaking with one of his friends about his faith and ended up leading him to Jesus.

Alex's friend hated Math's lessons and especially the regular Math's tests that his teacher imposed. He just never seemed to grasp any of the subject. On a good day he scraped a pass, but most days he failed. As they were talking about this the day before yet another test, Alex suggested they should pray. No adults were involved in the conversation – Alex hadn't spoken to any adult for advice – he was just living out his way of life as he had been raised. When the test results came back his friend had passed comfortably for the first time ever. God had answered Alex's prayer.

Even though Alex was still young he knew exactly the kind of life God had called him to – that was the environment he had been raised in since he could remember. For him, this was not a miracle, it was just ordinary living. The Josiah Generation will know that they have been born to do great things for God. This is something that will be in them from their earliest of years, even from their time in the womb.

When Josiah was born he was not only the grandson of the current king of Judah, he immediately became the second in line to the throne. This conferred on him a level of privilege and responsibility that no one else in the kingdom had to carry, even those many years his senior.

For as long as he could remember, people would have been calling him "the future king". He would have known that this was his destiny. There was no need for endless meetings for careers advice – he hardly had to work – and regardless of what grades he got in his exams, he would always be an heir to the throne.

When Josiah was just six, his grandfather died and his father became the king. Suddenly Josiah stepped closer to his future call. He was now next in line to the throne.

Not only was he the heir but, as a child, his dad was the most powerful person in his world. Imagine a group of children standing around the palace courtyard having the standard argument that all children have at some point over whose dad is the greatest...

"My dad's better than your dad," one says.

"Well, my dad's stronger than your dad."

"Yeah? Well my dad earns more money than your dad!"

Then Prince Josiah turns up to join in the conversation. After that the conversation quickly ends. Everyone has to agree that his dad is the greatest in the kingdom of Judah.

"Your dad may be stronger, but you wouldn't have any food if it weren't for my dad ... Your dad may be cleverer, but my dad could put him in prison if he didn't like him ... My daddy is the best!"

Older children probably wouldn't even try to compare their dad to Prince Josiah's dad. Instead they could compare him to the kings of other nations, attempting to prove that perhaps he is not the most powerful dad "in the world", but either way, all would have to acknowledge Josiah's unique position due to his father's greatness.

This must have made for a child who was fully secure in himself when it came to presenting his opinions and making decisions. I am not talking about a blind disregard for those around, because as we will see later, King Josiah really cared for people, but in him there would be a strong sense of self-identity and a knowledge of what he was called to do that would permeate his whole attitude. People who are secure in their standing don't need to push themselves forward, they can simply stand strong, be themselves, and people will notice.

Secure in authority

In many organizations the "middle management" works hard to exert their authority. They are closer in terms of their authority to the people they are leading and more inclined to be aware of the insecurities of those under them. Sandwiched, as they are, between the workers and the senior executives leading the organisation, they often handle their authority awkwardly, or heavy-handedly. Senior managers, however, are usually more comfortable wielding their authority. They know their position and strive less to be noticed. They carry themselves in a way that lets others know they are in charge and people respond to them accordingly. They don't need to shout to be heard; when they speak their authority backs up their words. Of course, there are exceptions to these stereotypes, but the principle holds true: *the greater your authority, the less you need to exert yourself to be heard.*

In the same way God is raising up a whole generation who *know their authority in Him*. They walk in the understanding that God has given them this authority in order to enable them to fulfil His plans for their lives. It is not an authority that has any arrogance or seeks to dominate those around them, but one that empowers them to serve and help those around them. Neither do they need to worry about their own reputation, because they know God is watching out for them. Children who grow up understanding this will not be insecure in their relationship with God, but will grow up knowing the authority of their Heavenly Father as the King of kings. This will influence every aspect of their lives.

One young teenager was an only child living at home with his mum. Ben had never known his dad, but he had grown up in an environment where God was his Dad. As the Father to the fatherless, God had the final say in his life. One Christmas he desperately wanted a PlayStation, but family finances meant this was impossible. Mum simply told him to ask his Dad. One week before Christmas, Daddy God provided the money for a PlayStation from an unexpected source. Ben knew that his Heavenly Father was great. He had grown up with this knowledge and it was now a foundational stone in his life.

Raised in the right environment

Not only would Josiah have been aware of his position amongst his peers – the other children of the court – but he would have quickly developed a sense of authority over all those around him. As heir to the throne, all who came into contact with him were his future subjects. His nanny could not afford to be a cruel nanny for fear of her future. Indeed, she probably worked hard to gain favour with the child in preparation for a peaceful and prosperous retirement when he was king! After all, his grandfather King Manasseh had been a tyrant who had shed much innocent blood. People had lived in fear of him and his ways. Who was to know how this young prince would turn out?

Josiah's teachers would have been the best available and he would have been accustomed to high standards of service. All would have been aware that, as future king, it would be better to be remembered by him pleasantly or not at all. Crossing the young prince was not an option. Even if he did not complain to the king about them then, he could easily initiate a vendetta against them once he came to power.

So everyone around Josiah would have treated him with care. His life as a child was one of immense privilege. You can't imagine him needing to see a counsellor because he did not feel special. He knew he was special! And his courtiers had a responsibility to ensure that he was prepared for his future role as king, with all the responsibility and authority that comes with such a role.

In the same way, parents, children's leaders and pastors all have a responsibility to see that this generation grows up knowing their God. Alongside homework, feeding, fun, washing, cleaning, rushing to school and back again, we need to keep our children's future destiny at the forefront of our minds – just as King Josiah's courtiers would have done. By this, I don't mean their destiny as doctors, lawyers or some other position of standing in the community we might hope they achieve, but their destiny as people who have a position of standing before God to influence change and see the kingdom of God grow in their time.

As we invest in our children's spiritual lives we are preparing the next generation to fulfil God's mandate. I often think of John Wesley's parents. Both were prayerful and taught their children from the Bible. Nobody really knows what they sowed into their children's lives, yet in their family they bred one of the world's greatest revivalists and one of the greatest hymn writers of all time.

The environment in which we place this Josiah Generation, both at home and in the church, is vital in developing them and helping them to fulfil God's call on their lives. Young children are spiritual beings, just like adults, and we have a duty to nurture them as ones who will be reigning and doing great things for God. This is not to say that we don't allow children to be children – it is simply that we must ensure that their childhood takes place in an environment where the knowledge of God is rife.

They will know that they have been called of God and that their lives are going somewhere.

For this Josiah Generation it is our responsibility not only to understand the destiny that God has for them, but also to treat them as ones who are already walking in this destiny. The Josiah Generation will do great things, but they require the right foundation. A lot of this stems from our attitude towards them and our perception of their future.

I'm not cute, I'm powerful

One Sunday morning one of our leaders was working in the church crèche. A toddler there was singing a church song. As the girl sang the song, she lifted her hands in the same way she had sometimes seen the adults do in church. The leader thought to herself, "Ah, she is so cute."

Immediately she heard an audible voice: "Don't!"

She turned around to see who had spoken and saw no one there. She turned back to look at the little girl and heard the voice once more: "Don't despise these little ones, for this is holy ground." She understood God was speaking to her.

Once we understand the call that God has placed on the Josiah Generation, it changes our whole view of the young children in our churches. As the Psalmist says in Psalm 8:2 (NIV), *"From the lips of children and infants* [not teenagers], *you have ordained praise because of your enemies, to silence the foe and the avenger."* To put it another way: when babies and toddlers praise God (and they will because He has ordered it), Satan has to keep quiet. That is high level spiritual warfare at work!

Children are not simply cute, they are powerful. If we limit their spiritual actions by labelling them "cute", we are degrading the call that is on their lives. Instead we should prize, nurture and encourage their relationship with God. Sometimes crèches are thought of and run simply as places to keep children occupied and expose them to a few Bible stories, while "real church" takes place elsewhere. But God, who has seen these children in the womb and known them before the foundations of the earth, is watching over them and is busy preparing them for their future. Even their times in the crèche can and should be a key time in their spiritual lives where they experience God. Our crèches are not meant to be glorified babysitting services where we look after the children so that the adults can get on with proper church. Instead they should be ministry arenas where God is allowed to meet with these little ones. As Jesus said in Matthew 19:14, we are to let the little ones come to Him without hindrance, for the kingdom of heaven belongs to such as these.

Viewed from this perspective, serving in the crèche is not simply a duty that needs to be performed by someone, it is an honour God has given to us and an important opportunity to serve Him. Just as King Josiah's servants would have been handpicked with care, so we should be careful to choose the most prayerful, godly people to work with our babies. Just as we would expect the preacher on a Sunday morning to pray and prepare for his ministry to the adults, so we should pray and prepare for the ministry within our crèche programmes.

A new song

One evening I gathered my key leaders around me to share with them a new song God had given me just before the weekend. I was so excited because it was the first song we had written for the babies and I knew that it was a special God-song.

I sang it to the group and everyone was excited – everyone, that is, except for the leader of the crèche ministry. She just stood there with a strange look on her face. I have to be honest, it was quite off-putting to sing this song with that face looking at me, but I was sure the song was from God so chose to ignore it. When I came to the end, everyone was deeply moved.

Finally the crèche leader spoke: "Last Sunday it was crazy in the crèche. All the children were crying and a few were trying to fight. We tried praying, we tried distracting the children with other activities, but nothing was working. It was one of the worst Sundays ever. But then, one little girl started to say "Jesus, Jesus, Jesus," over and over again. She ended with "Jesus loves us every day." She then started to repeat the name of Jesus ending with, "Jesus loves us every week." She repeated it again, this time ending with "Jesus loves us every year." By this time, all the children had calmed down and the place went quiet. Then, in the silence, she sang exactly the same song that you have just shared with us."

All of us on the team knew that this was a holy moment. As we raise the Josiah Generation we should expect God to meet with these children from a young age, and for them to be fully tuned into the voice of their Father.

Knowing their heritage

As a child, Josiah would have been taught the history of his nation. He was one of the last kings to reign in Judah before it was thrust into exile and the kingly lineage can be traced all the way back to his far off relative, King David. One of his other relatives was King Solomon, who even today is remembered as the wisest king. Solomon's reputation would have made an impression on the young king's mind.

Every stream of Christian tradition has a rich heritage of God moving among His people. As we share our history with our children, we encourage them to anticipate their future more eagerly. When our children know something of what God has done around them, they are more ready for what God is going to do through them.

One child was challenged at school about how he knew God existed. In one of his classes the teacher said to him, "God isn't real, so why do you think He is?" The child shot straight back: "Firstly, I have met Him and secondly He healed my mum from cancer." The teacher could give no reply; this child knew his heritage.

Confident in their calling

We have noted that as a young child, Josiah would have understood something of his authority long before he had to carry the burden of the responsibilities that came with that authority. He didn't have to stop and ask himself, "Do I have the right to tell the people around me what to do?" He knew he had that authority and expected to function in it.

The Josiah Generation is growing up with an understanding that God is there and He is real. They also understand that God has given them a responsibility to serve the world around them and to make a difference. Imagine a whole army of children confident that God is on their side, not worrying about whether He will answer them, but more concerned to know whether they are doing what He wants of them. This is not so much something that can be taught, it's an attitude that is caught.

Many times when a new teacher starts working with children they begin by hoping that the children will listen to what they say. They ask the group to sit down and hope their instructions will be followed. More experienced teachers understand their authority. They no longer hope the children will listen, instead they expect the children to listen. The whole tone and attitude that they speak with means the children do listen. They have crossed the line from hoping for a response to expecting one.

In the same way, the Josiah Generation will have crossed the line at a young age from *hoping* God is there to *knowing* God is really in charge and He's also their Daddy. The Josiah Generation will grow up knowing that they have access to God's great authority because of their relationship with Him. It is not something they will have reason to doubt – it is simply something they will learn to use. This knowledge comes from the environment that they are raised in. As they see those around them trusting God to answer their prayers, they will do the same and experience God for themselves at a young age.

In short, Prince Josiah was in training for reigning. The same sense of destiny hangs over this up-and-coming generation. They are being raised for a purpose. As we understand their future call we can be a key link in the chain preparing them for that call.

3

Reigning From An Early Age

"Josiah was eight years old when he became king,
and he reigned thirty-one years in Jerusalem."
(2 Kings 22:1)

Living out their destiny

Rachel was 8 years old. She had been at our church for most of her life and had been looking forward to the day when she could become a leader. After some leadership training and a lot of prayer she started to tell her friends about Jesus.

Before long Rachel had started her own group in her school. Every week she came back with stories of more people joining the group until eventually she was leading a group of fifteen children her age. God was definitely up to something, working through her.

One day I sat with her to find out more about how her group was doing and to check that it was not simply a social group, but that she really was leading her friends to Jesus. I was looking for any weakness in her leadership so that I could help to develop her and encourage her in the work that she was doing.

She started by telling me how she prayed for her cell each day and prepared things to teach them from the Bible. They were spending time in prayer together and worshiped God together each week and she ended each meeting by delivering a challenge for her friends to tackle in the week ahead. All in all she was doing a great job, leading her group at a very high standard. I was just about to encourage her when she carried on...

"After the meeting some of the group come to me and share their problems and I pray with them." I was thrilled by this clear indication that the group, most of whom she had led to Jesus herself, saw her as their spiritual leader. It was real confirmation that she was doing a great job. But before I could tell her that she kept on speaking:

"Then next week I follow up with them to see if the problem is better. If it is, then we thank God because He has done a miracle. If not, then I pray again until it is."

By this time I was greatly moved. We always knew this eight-year old had a pastor's heart for people and now, through her ministry, she was showing it. I felt gently rebuked for the times when I have failed to follow people up as I should due to the busyness of life. Here she was ministering to the flock God had given her better than me. The whole point of this conversation had been to develop her. Instead, I was being challenged.

Once I had recovered my composure I went on to ask her more. "So when you follow this up with people, if God has done a miracle do you share this with the rest of the group?" Rachel looked at me and paused for a moment before she spoke. "It depends. I ask the person and see if they are happy for me to share with the rest of the group. If they are, then we tell them, but if not we don't."

I was left speechless. The wisdom of God working through the life of an eight-year old never ceases to amaze me.

Ice cream on demand

King Josiah, just like Rachel, began reigning at the age of eight. It was far earlier than the people responsible for his development had anticipated. His father had only been king for two years before his officials assassinated him. Those officials were then killed by the people who went on to make Josiah king.

So when Josiah became king it was not only much earlier than expected, but none of his father's officials were around to assist him. The palace would have been filled with new people, all of who were finding their feet in their new roles. Yet King Josiah, young though he was, would have been comfortable with this new reign. After all, he had thought about it constantly, especially in the last two years since his father had become king and he had become the next in line to the throne.

Of course, Josiah would not have been running the kingdom single handed. He had a staff of officials and advisors to do most of the work for him. Yet, they were still *his* staff. If one day Josiah wanted an ice cream in the middle of winter, which of his courtiers could refuse him? Someone would immediately have been dispatched to go and make one for him, knowing that their success, even in a task as trivial as this, could affect their future prospects for promotion. From Josiah's point of view, his ability to give a command and see it executed immediately had been with him from an early age. The fact of his authority was ingrained in him and he was learning to use it with care.

Today's children are in a similar position to King Josiah. They have an opportunity to begin to carry things in the Spirit from an early age. Little children are always welcome to come to God and so their prayers carry the same authority as ours — namely God's authority — to bring about answers. They have a great life of service ahead of them.

One time, the great revivalist D.L. Moody held a crusade. When he returned a friend asked him how it had gone. "Not bad," he replied. "Two and a half people got saved."

His friend looked quizzically, "What do you mean two and a half? Do you mean two adults and one child?"

"No, I mean two children and one adult," he responded. "The adult has already lived half their life and only has half left in which to serve God. Whereas the children have their whole lives ahead of them in which they can serve God."

How much better for children to begin to serve God now and continue to live for Him through their teenage years and on into adulthood, rather than coming to know Him as young adults and then needing several years to unlearn all the ways of the world they have been raised in, before being ready for leadership service in God's kingdom.

Of course, a child on their own can't do anything of significance in God's kingdom, but then nor can an adult. Both require God to work alongside them for anything to take place. Great exploits for God's kingdom happen because of the great God working through willing servants. But if children are willing, then God can and will work through them. It is not as if children receive a baby version of the Holy Spirit and so can only do baby things for God until they are older. No, they receive the *fullness of God*. They can, therefore, have both the ability and the desire to serve Him while they are still young.

So there comes a time when children move from being prepared for ministry to being given opportunities to minister. In all of this we are not talking about raising up some freak generation who are so spiritual that they cannot live in the real world. Far from being strange, they will be *strangely normal*. The closer they get to God, the more radical they will be concerning His kingdom. The more childlike they remain, the more they will grow to be whole individuals. And once whole and secure in their knowledge of God, they can blossom in every area of their lives. Over the years I have delighted in seeing the children closest to God stand out as the most normal among the group, simply being who God has made them to be.

My children could never do that

Reading some of these stories about the Josiah Generation, some may look at the children around them and think, "My children could never do that." And in a way they are right. Josiah was only ready to be king because his preparation began at an early age. He was raised in the right environment, surrounded by people who understood the call on his life and lived to facilitate it.

Ultimately, there are no limits to what God can do through children (or adults), but the Josiah Generation require something from us to help them to fulfil their call. Our role is to give them opportunities to connect with God. Even the youngest of children can be impacted by God while they are under our care, and this should surely be one of the goals we have for the babies and children who are in our family and attend our church.

One of our children in the crèche was two years old. He had been coming since he was born. When Mum fell pregnant, Dad walked out on her and through the trauma of it all she discovered God. Her love for God was evident as He helped her through those hard times. Her son, Adam, was clearly a special boy and from the moment he was born the mother invested a lot of time and prayer into him, wanting a better life for him then she herself had experienced up to that point.

When Adam was a couple of years old his dad came back on the scene. Dad was resistant to the gospel so Mum stopped trying to convert him, choosing instead to let him see the change in her for himself. In turn, Dad was keen to be a good father after his years of neglect and so was seeking to win back favour with his wife and make up for lost time building a relationship with his son. As a result, every night he volunteered to read the bedtime story.

Every night Adam asked him to read from a toddler's Bible. Night after night this went on. Dad kept suggesting other books, "Are you sure you don't want Thomas the Tank Engine or Winnie the Pooh?"

"No! Bible, Bible!" Adam always asserted.

Before long, through the simplicity of the toddler's Bible, Dad came to know the Lord and went on to become a very active member of the church. God had used a two-year old to lead his father to Christ. Christ in a child has the power to bring change and to speak words of righteousness. As we continue to connect children to Jesus, moving from simply teaching them about God to training them in His ways, we will see many similar, amazing things happen – not just while they are children, but also in their future lives.

The leaders of today

Over the past few decades children's ministry has undergone many radical changes in the Western world. Initially, people saw children simply as the future church. With this attitude, a renewed emphasis was placed on teaching children directly from the Bible. After all, if they were to be the future church, then we should start to prepare them for that future by imparting to them a knowledge of God's Word in a way that was accessible to them.

Many children's leaders spoke up during this shift of thinking and fought for children to be recognised as "full" members of the church now, not simply as a group of people standing in the wings waiting to join in. So children became known as the church of today and the church of tomorrow. Children needed to be nurtured in the Lord because of their position in the church. This meant more than simply teaching them Bible stories: they needed to be given opportunities to worship God for themselves.

Once this principle was established, people began to realise that in many ways ministry to children was even more valuable than ministry to adults, since children were not only the church of today, but the leaders of tomorrow. This revolution led to a whole new emphasis being placed on the importance of investing into the lives of children to ensure that there would be a healthy leadership for future generations.

With the dawn of the Josiah Generation, however, children are not just the church of today and the leaders of tomorrow … *they are leaders in the church both today and tomorrow.*

I am not talking, of course, about children running their own churches or bearing responsibility for things like the legal aspects of running a charity, health and safety compliance, or conducting marriage counselling. They still need adults around them to help and guide them. But, they can be equally used by God to help others to know Him. They can, and indeed should, be leading others to God.

Often we don't see children in this way. Perhaps we see that they make the occasional God-inspired comment here and there which makes us stop and think, but we assume this was more a random moment than a glimpse into their destiny. Yet, if we nurture this aspect of their lives then we will see them grow and develop to the point where they can be used powerfully by God.

Children are growing and developing in so many different ways. This growth requires them to develop the skills and be given the opportunities necessary for them to reach their full potential. Take a simple example like getting dressed. Newborn babies simply do not have the skills to dress themselves, but as they grow into toddlers they develop the coordination to be able to put on some of their clothes. Developing coordination is not enough, though – they also need to be given the opportunity to practice. Opportunity, given at the right stage of development with the right support, leads to children thriving in any area.

This is the balance that God loves to have as He develops His people. Deuteronomy 32:11 speaks of this type of development:

"…an eagle stirs up its nest, hovers over its young, spreading out its wings, taking them up, carrying them on its wings…"

We know that the eagle pushes its chicks out of the nest, but then swoops down to catch them. The eagle gives its chicks the opportunity to fly, whilst all the while being ready to catch and support them at the slightest sign of danger. The eagle repeats this process over and over again until the chicks learn to fly on their own. In the same way children need both opportunity and support if they are to blossom in their role as spiritual leaders.

We have found that as we encourage children to begin to speak to their friends, some will speak to only one or two, while others will tell their whole class. Each child rises to the level they are ready for. The responsibility is on us to see that children are not only given opportunities to develop as spiritual leaders, as King Josiah was, but that they are also encouraged to take up those opportunities – with us standing next to them, ready to support them.

If you have a pack of seeds, those seeds will never grow whilst they are kept in the packet. Instead you have to plant them into pots and ensure they receive the right amount of heat and water in the right season of the year. For this generation to fulfil their calling as ones who are to influence those around them, we have to plant the seed of spiritual leadership and be there to support it so that it can grow. When the time is right, the children will flourish in their service of God. Every child is unique, so for different children this will happen at different times and in different ways.

The Josiah Generation are called to lead from an early age. This requires sensitivity on our part to release them into their destiny. The core of our work with the children in our family and our church should be to prepare them to be leaders who will influence those around them for God's kingdom.

4

Different to Their Fathers

"[Josiah] did what was right in the sight of the LORD, and walked in all the ways of his father David; he did not turn aside to the right hand or to the left."

(2 Kings 22:2)

My parents let me go to church

Albert had led one of his friends, Mahir, to the Lord. This was significant because Mahir's parents were devout followers of another religion. It had all happened in the school playground one day and since then they had been meeting regularly to talk about God and pray together. Top of the prayer agenda was how to tell Mahir's parents.

In the end they didn't have to tell his parents as they found out anyway. Mahir was expecting to be banned from ever speaking to Albert again, but somehow in a God-moment the opposite happened. His parents linked the drastic improvement in his behaviour, and the recent rise in his school grades, with his change in religion. Against every norm for their religious culture they gave him permission, not just to continue learning about God, but also to attend church.

As our church was quite far from where he lived, Mahir began attending one all by himself that was walking distance from his house. And he kept on attending. Mahir had separated himself from his parent's religion and was taking a different path from his ancestors. Mahir is a part of the Josiah Generation.

King Josiah stood apart from his father and his grandfather. From a young age he devoted his life to following God's plan, even though both the kings in his life who had ruled before him had rejected outright the same plan in their reign. Manasseh, his grandfather, had undone the good work of his godly predecessor, Hezekiah. Manasseh re-built the high places and altars and once again worshipped the false gods of the people who Joshua and King David had worked so hard to evict centuries earlier.

The lives of both Josiah's grandfather, King Manasseh, and his father, King Amon, can be summed up by the oft-repeated biblical phrase: "ones who did evil in the sight of the Lord." Manasseh reigned for fifty-five years and his evil was truly astounding. He was likened to the king of evil, King Ahab, and he led Israel back into the ways of the Amorites, who had been evicted from the land because of their evil. Similarly, King Amon was so evil that his courtiers assassinated him after only two years on the throne.

Josiah, then, had been brought up in a place of tyranny – the son of a tyrant with all the power that comes from such a position.

Yet King Josiah chose to be different.

He chose to live another way. Somehow he had separated from the ways of his known relatives to reconnect with the ways of King David and the patriarchs of old.

Josiah could have been more extreme in renouncing the ways of his fathers. He could have gone one step further and renounced the throne altogether. If he was uncomfortable with the ways of reigning he had witnessed, he could have chosen to reject everything about being king. Knowing how badly his predecessors had carried out their duties, he could have labelled the entire function of kingship as "evil". The easiest way for him to avoid being a bad king himself, and possibly bringing destruction to the lives of his subjects, would perhaps be to abdicate the throne and go and live the life of a hermit, serving God in solitude.

This is the attitude that some believers have taken, rejecting their role in the world in favour of pursuing alternatives ways of serving God. But by burying their heads in the sand so they can "focus on serving God", they actually miss the service that He is calling them to. Some have gone further still and have rejected their role in the church because they see some of the failings of the established church of today. In doing so, they have thrown out the baby with the bath water. Rather than being instruments of change they have added to the problems of the church.

But King Josiah did not reject his kingship. Instead, although he understood his recent heritage, he was determined to rule differently. The freedom and privilege of leadership was something that he neither rejected nor abused. It was something he chose to use for the purposes of God.

In the same way, the Josiah Generation will not shirk their responsibilities in the church or the world, but will be able to separate from the ungodly ways of their forefathers and live above the standards of the world they are raised in. For some, like Mahir, this could involve a rejection of their entire upbringing, requiring a complete change of worldview. But even for those raised in Christian homes, there will be a "separation" that will be more subtle, but just as significant for the future of the church.

Like King Josiah this generation will not reject their position in the church, but will use it to bring about a restoration of the church. God will give this generation a special grace to be able to reject the stale traditions of church, whilst not rejecting the concept of church. Even the most radical churches still have some way to go before the whole body can be described as the bride of Christ, but the Josiah Generation will help to propel the church towards its destiny.

My Pastor has banned me from church

One Sunday I stood up in front of a group of our children as their pastor and formally banned every single one of them from going to church. There was an audible gasp; you could see the children were confused. The other adults in the room were also concerned. Their thoughts were visible on their faces: "Perhaps the pastor has made a mistake ... maybe he has finally lost it!"

So I repeated myself for dramatic effect: "You are banned from going to church..."

"...I no longer want you to *go* to church. Instead I want you to start to *be* the church!"

People "go to church" every Sunday and then "leave the church" and go home doing nothing different. The very language we use to talk about the church reinforces this concept as each Sunday we "go to" church and then "come home from" church. Yet God calls us to be the church, to be salt and light in the world. We are to be church and meet together as church.

As the next generation rejects the traditions we have held dear, challenging times lie ahead for many of us occupying the older generations. Jesus challenged the Pharisees that their love for their own traditions superseded their love for God – and many reacted with anger. The fact is, we may be blind to our traditions until this generation challenges them. At that moment it will be a test of our Christian maturity to see how we respond to their challenge.

When children outrun their parents

I have seen children who were more passionate for God than their parents and this presented a dilemma for the parents who brought them to church. Incredibly, a few sought to squash their children's passion (we will only go to church when we feel like it). Many have accommodated their children's desires (okay, you can go to this event to meet with God). But some have allowed their children's fire to challenge them in their personal walk with God.

One parent came to tell me how her child's prayer life had so challenged her that she had had to step up a gear in prayer. Another spoke of how her child's Bible knowledge had put her to shame and it made her study the Bible more deeply.

One day God told a boy called Joshua to read through the book of Revelation. He immediately obeyed and was gripped by what he read. As he was in the car with his family he suddenly blurted out, "Mummy, what does God mean when He says in Revelation 21:8 that cowards and unbelievers and the others will be thrown into the lake of fire?" Once the mum had recovered from the depth of the question, she double checked that the reference he had given her was right (for which she had to use a Bible) and then explained the verse that had been going round her six-year-old's head in a way that he could understand.

Once children meet with God they want more of Him. In the south of France there is a delicious cake called a "Tarte Tropezienne". It looks like an ordinary cake, but once you have had one bite you just have to have a bit more! You taste a bit and it evokes a desire for more. The same is true of God (just without the negative side effects of calories and rotting teeth!)

That is why children who have met with God keep coming back. Spiritual life is ignited on the inside of them and they hunger for more of Him. They taste and see that God is good. I have seen this in some of the comments parents have passed on to me:

"We left the church, but our child insisted we came back."

"We had to change our flights because our child was so upset we would be missing the special worship event."

"My child insists that they have to go on the weekend away to meet with God, but we can't afford it. Can you help?"

"A few months ago we moved house and so began attending a different church, but they just weren't happy there. They wanted to meet with God so we've decided to come back, even though it will mean travelling over an hour each week."

"Our child won't let us miss a week of church even for one weekend. We have to plan our whole lives around meeting with God."

(Isn't that what being a Christian is all about? Planning our whole lives around God!)

Of course, not every child will develop this hunger in a group at the same rate. That's where the prayers of the leaders and parents come in to cover those children whose light has not yet switched on. But once it has, there will be no turning back. There may be tough times where they need our support, but they will never doubt once they have met God.

Graham was a lovely boy from a very rough estate in London. He came on a God weekend and left visibly changed. Everyone on the estate knew that he had met God. One day he was just about to enter a friend's house when he heard his friend shouting and cursing his mum. The child's mother did not know what to do or how to respond. This was a growing problem that she could not get on top of; she had lost her parental authority. Graham waded in and rebuked his friend who in turn apologised to his mum. Blessed are the peacemakers. Graham had separated from the ways of many on the estate, choosing to follow God instead.

Selina was a fiery girl. She longed to see God move in her school that was linked with the Church of England. But it seemed like every attempt she made was thwarted. The school leadership opposed the gospel, fearing it would offend the significant proportion of Muslims who attended, even though a survey of the Muslim parents showed that they had actually chosen to send their children to the school because they wanted them to be exposed to Christian values and teachings.

Eventually, the head teacher agreed to allow a Christian assembly to take place during Easter. Her expectation had been for a pleasant, traditional service, singing a couple of hymns and not rocking the boat. However, Selina was given permission to organise it and somehow she brought in a band and a Christian rap artist. She also preached the gospel and shared her testimony.

Though the head teacher wasn't happy about this, the staff and pupils loved it. Selina had separated from the leadership over her in order to line up with her destiny as a believer.

Get ready

In the same way, King Josiah was able to separate himself from his upbringing, whilst still holding on to the general direction that he had been raised in – to rule over the kingdom. The Josiah Generation will do the same, returning to the very foundations of church.

Every godly leader desires this and works towards it, but it takes a move of God for it to happen.

God is preparing the Josiah Generation for that very move. They will return to the roots of the early church, overstepping every church tradition that has been established as the norm. They will be extreme in getting back to God's norm.

This goes against the grain of our modern society and indeed, many aspects of this generation will go against the grain of both the world and the church as it is now. As they separate from the ways of their predecessors it may seem to some like a division, but in truth it is a union with God and His plans. As John Lake said, "Principle is better than unity, but the end result of principle will be unity."

When we see this generation standing up for the truth, we will have a choice as to how we respond. We could squash this seed of reformation in them, we could passively stand by and see if it grows, or we could allow it to challenge us in our walk with God. Of course, the closer we are to God's norm the less challenge there will be, and the more we will be willing to flow with it. This will be the key issue that the preceding generations will have to face as the Josiah Generation steps up into its destiny.

5

Seeking God Young

"In the eighth year of his reign, while [Josiah] was still young, he began to seek the God of his father David."
(2 Chronicles 34:3)

We want God

A number of the youth who had moved on from the children's ministry came to us to complain. "We want God. We don't just want social meetings, we want to meet with God." Since they were young, they had been familiar with seeking God and meeting with Him, and now as they were growing to be more aware of the world around them, they wanted new opportunities and ways to seek God. The youth leader began to give them these opportunities.

For hours at a time some could be lost in worship. Others met for a band practice which, when they had finished, led into a prayer time. Before long, the youth band were on their knees crying out to God.

Something was stirring inside of them.

King Josiah went through a similar thing. At the age of 16 the Bible simply states that he began to seek God. This simple phrase is describing something beyond simply following a tradition – it speaks more of that hunger for God that can only be satisfied by time with Him. The Psalmist captures this desire in Psalm 42:

"Just like the deer thirsts for water, so I am thirsty for you."

God consumes every thought and directs every action. The whole of the world is seen from God's viewpoint and priorities are set accordingly.

As members of the Josiah Generation grow, they will want more of God. This desire for God will bring about profound changes in them.

One meeting changes you

We'd taken some young teenagers away for the weekend. Among the group was one young lady whose attitude was palpable. She had enough makeup on to cover a whole dance troupe and she clearly was not bowled over at the idea of spending a weekend with a bunch of folks from church. Her face looked like she was ready to start a fight given the slightest provocation and she gave off a vibe that meant most people steered clear of her. Put simply, she was a hurting teenager.

Over the course of the weekend her words, her actions and even her body language expressed this hurt. But on the final day she looked different. She came downstairs in the morning wearing no makeup and stood in front of the whole group. There she shared how she had met with God in the session the previous evening. God had spoken to her and told her how beautiful she was on the inside. Now she didn't feel the need to wear makeup to make herself beautiful. Not only was she free of cosmetics, but more significantly she was free on the inside. All the other youngsters in the group were shocked at the visible change in her face, as her anger and her attitude had been changed by God.

One meeting with God is all it takes to bring about radical change.

A couple of brothers were causing their mum real problems. They destroyed furniture in the home and when they were at school they were no better. After meeting with God at the weekend they both went to school on Monday with a different attitude.

Mum was so excited with the change until half way through Monday when she came down to earth with a bump. She received a phone call from the school: "You need to come and speak to us at the end of school," the teacher said. This was a familiar phone call and she was not looking forward to the meeting. It usually led to a complaint regarding her youngest son's poor behaviour, and the disruption and damage caused to property or another pupil.

As she walked into her son's classroom the teacher who had called her was waiting. On seeing her the teacher leapt up. "What has happened to your child? He has gone from the worst pupil to the best overnight; from the most disruptive to the most helpful. In all my years of teaching I have never seen such a change take place in such a short space of time. I need to know what he did this weekend."

With a sigh of relief, his mother was able to share about the profound encounter he had had with God.

An encounter with God brings about change. As children open themselves up to God, what they encounter in His presence brings about a change that is positive – that ignites inside them a hunger for more of Him. And once the hunger for God is there, there is no turning back. Things that seemed important fade into the background. Tensions between their life at church and their life at school or college melt away as one driving passion consumes them – a passion for God.

Jean-Samuel had been raised in a stable home. He loved God with all his heart. As he moved into his teenage years something new was ignited inside of him. As he worshipped God he would lift his hands and the whole room would be filled with the tangible presence of God. Jean-Samuel was seeking God at a deeper level than he ever had before. All those around him wanted to be like him because they saw how different he was. Jean-Samuel was a leader among leaders in Gods' kingdom.

All this focus on God's kingdom does not mean that children and young people will drop out of regular life. Of course, they don't suddenly stop doing their homework because they are completely taken up with God. In fact, my observation has been that the more they put God first in their lives, the more their grades improve. Neither does it mean that they no longer hang out with their school friends. Indeed, their school friends often want to be around them and become like them. It just means that there is one thing that they allow, even require, to influence every aspect of their lives – their relationship with God.

As they come to this age it is as if God sees that they are now ready to fully handle the spiritual responsibility that He has for them, so He opens up a new level of His presence to them. As their brains and emotions have developed enough to be able to handle Him at this new level, they are ready to influence not only those around them, but even those unknown to them.

To put it another way: they are no longer children, they are now "grown up" in the kingdom of God. They understand their need for Him and this becomes the driving desire of their lives. As children they were surrounded by godly influences and moved in the flow of God all their lives, serving Him as opportunities arose. As teenagers they now begin to seek God aggressively.

I don't have the space here to speak of the many I know who, as they grew, discovered the presence of God at a new level and found the power of God working through them in a new way. These are young people who learned the power of prayer as they reached out to their friends at school and not only led them to the Lord, but helped them to grow in the things of God.

Now in their teens and desperately hungry for more of God, some will look at them and think they have become extreme. But "extreme" is part of the very makeup of all teenagers. Young people will see visions so clearly that they want to make them a reality immediately and driven by youthful energy and blissfully ignorant of the possibility of failure they can accomplish much. Better to be like this than like the many young people who are drifting through life because they have nothing to be extreme about. The great thing about being extreme for God is that it brings an incredible balance to every area of life, since everything is now seen from the right perspective.

Time to seek Him

One day we were running a special event for the children in the church and the teenagers wanted to be a part of it. We could have asked them to help with registration or even toilet runs, but we knew that God had been stirring them to seek Him, so we threw out a challenge for them to pray for the event whilst it was going on.

We found a small room in the church that was available and opened it up to them. On the day of the event around 20 young teenagers gathered, with no adult present, and started to pray. As they prayed the room got hotter and hotter (both spiritually and physically as the windows in that room could not be opened). Some of the teenagers were prophesying over the event, others cried out to God for salvation. Upstairs, where the children were, God's presence was tangible as the teenagers called Him down from above. They prayed for around 90 minutes in the room we later named "the boiler room" – the spiritual hot house for the ministry. These teenagers under our care had transitioned from simply taking on board the spiritual food we were feeding them, to preparing "meals" for themselves from scratch.

At other times we have called together some of our children and young people who are preparing for leadership to pray for a prolonged period of several hours. The first time people participate in something like this, you can sense they feel a little unsure about whether they are going to live through the experience! But each time at the end the children make comments like, "Is that it? It felt like we were only here for a few minutes." As they discover the power of prayer in God's presence, a flame is ignited on the inside of them to pray more.

One day I was showing a visitor around our ministry base. We stopped to chat to a young leader called Laetitia. She was not quite a teenager, but was leading her friends to Jesus and doing great work for the kingdom. The visitor asked a few questions about her leadership and what she was doing in her school. Then she asked the key question: "How long do you pray for each day?" Laetitia paused and replied honestly: "I don't know. I just wake up, pray, and then go to school."

With a few more questions we worked out that she was spending close to a couple of hours praying to God each morning. She was nearly late for school some days because she was so busy praying. This is the new generation that God is raising up.

Lighting the fire

One weekend we had taken away some young men as part of a boys-to-men programme. This "wilderness weekend" was designed to push them to the limits of responsibility. Among other tasks they had to cook their own food on an open fire. One night we decided to have a huge camp fire.

One boy in particular, Emmanuel, had taken a real fancy to starting fires. He came ready to get it started and we worked together with him. It took about an hour to get going, but once it started we piled on huge tree trunks. The flames were so high and the heat so hot that we had to sit several metres away from the fire for it to be bearable (let alone comfortable).

At the end, some of the young people threw pots of water over the fire to put it out, but it was too strong that the water just turned into steam. The next morning the fire was still burning so strongly that we were able to use it to cook our breakfast. It would have continued indefinitely as long as more fuel was added.

This is the kind of fiery passion that God is igniting inside the Josiah Generation – an unquenchable passion to seek Him; a fire that is enduring and contagious. As we recognise what God is doing in this generation we can act as a catalyst to release them into seeking God in a radical way, for God has a great plan for this generation.

As King Josiah sought God this was the trigger for everything else that he accomplished in his life. We can fan the flame of desire for God in the lives of young people and once it is going, even if others try to extinguish it, it will continue to burn strong. God has placed a desire in them to seek Him and the Josiah Generation is responding willingly.

6
Purging the High Places

"In the twelfth year [of his reign, Josiah] *began to purge Judah and Jerusalem of the high places, the wooden images, the carved images and the molded images."*
(2 Chronicles 34:3)

Time for a change in culture

A group of teenage girls had come together for Sunday church and were sitting around complaining:

"It's awful."

"They shouldn't be allowed to get away with it."

"I know, my younger sister saw it with me; she should never have been allowed to see it."

"Yeah, it was way before the watershed."

They were all talking about a television advert they had seen, aired on a music channel, that had shocked them. Their discernment receptors had gone into overdrive and now they wanted to make a stand for godliness. They needed to take action. Their leader mentioned that they could write a letter of complaint if they felt that strongly about it and that is exactly what they did.

Several months later the official body gave its verdict. They judged that the station had been wrong to show that clip when they did and the girls' complaint was upheld. In coming to this decision, the governing body noted that the majority of complaints had come from young people. Since then, the station has been fined substantial amounts because of its repeated failings in continuing to broadcast inappropriate content.

God used these teenagers to initiate change in the community.

King Josiah started his own programme of reform – one that would be the most radical the nation of Judah had ever seen. He began to tear down the idolatrous "high places" wherever he saw them. He sought out every tribute to a false god and ensured that it was removed. His reforms were so radical that they would have unsettled the multitude of people. He was presenting them with a very clear choice: *worship the true God or don't worship at all.*

2 Kings 23:4-7 tells us that King Josiah began in the temple, removing the idols that had somehow snuck their way in there. Parts of the temple had become so desecrated that male shrine prostitutes and women weaving for Asherah had set up residence there. Josiah simply tore down their dwelling places.

They were not just evicted without notice, their homes were destroyed at the same time. This may not have rocked the boat too much. After all, Josiah was king of Judah which was supposed to be following the God of Israel, and the temple was supposed to be the focal point of worship for Him. Even those who had forgotten about God would understand the logic of what Josiah was doing: if the temple was devoted to one God, then it was not too radical to insist that only the worship of God took place there.

But Josiah's reforms were not confined to the temple.

Outside the walls of the church building

One day we took some young people on a mission to a small market town. The young people had each prayed to God asking to hear from Him about someone they would meet that day and they had written letters to those people. They had also prepared cookies with simple messages from God on them to hand out to anyone who wanted them. Each missionary was wearing a T-shirt with a message on it that they had heard from God. They were ready to make a difference.

As the team set out we were very aware that either God was going to be in what we were doing or we were going to look very silly. We'd been deliberating between two different places to go to, both near each other, but felt God leading us to one in particular.

At the very entrance to the village was a spiritualist church and you could feel a cold chill as you passed the building where God was not glorified. You could feel the oppression in the town, but God had sent us on this mission. We had not even stepped off the bus when one of the teenagers saw the lady God had spoken to him about as he had prayed earlier that day – she looked exactly the same as the vision that God had given him, down to the clothes she was wearing, the things she was doing and the people who were around her! God was clearly in this.

We continued speaking with people through the afternoon and having great fun serving God, giving out cookies to surprised strangers and blessing those who we came into contact with. One small child took a cookie and walked off reading the words on it again and again: "Jesus is Lord, Jesus is Lord." As Psalm 8:2 says, when the children praise God the enemy is silenced. Change was beginning in that community.

God did many wonderful things that day, but we did not fully understand the significance of what was happening until a local pastor approached us. He explained how they had done many outreaches on the streets of the nearby town, but whenever they had tried to do anything here, for one reason and another it just did not happen. He was thrilled to see the gospel being proclaimed on the streets and we sensed that we had been present at the start of something new in that place, breaking open new ground through our actions.

The work of the Josiah Generation is not confined within the walls of a building. God is calling them to be the church wherever they go. Josiah was a radical king throughout his life and reign. He did not simply stop at reforming the temple, he began to tear down every focal point for idolatrous worship. His reforms spread through every corner of his kingdom.

You can imagine his advisors being a bit nervous about the changes he was bringing. After all, there would have been many devoted followers of the various religions and Josiah was doing his level best to offend all of them. He was not restrained by political correctness. Rather he was constrained by his passion for God. Those around him may have felt unsettled, but Josiah was a king who knew how to carry his authority. He was a force to be reckoned with.

The Asherah poles would have been as well known then as various points of religious worship are in our society today. The removal of them was no small feat. Not only did Josiah have the boldness to remove them, he also had the perseverance to see the job through. There were numerous points set up all over the place. To remove all of them required a well-organised, clearly defined plan. Many other good kings before him had removed some of these idols, but Josiah was so zealous for God he removed them all.

Josiah was not performing a cosmetic job to please the crowds. He didn't simply pack the false altars away, he thoroughly destroyed them. He even burnt the bones of priests on the altars so that they could never be used again. In one fell swoop he removed the priests and completely desecrated the altars.

Josiah's reforms of Jerusalem were not enacted in some secret meeting, away from the glare of the "media" of his day. His actions would have made front page news in the equivalents of the tabloids and broadsheets of today. The high places where the altars were built were exactly that – high places, visible spots, landmarks for those around to see. Josiah was speaking out a loud "NO" to idol worship, so clearly that no one had any doubt about what he believed. They could choose to disagree, but his actions were so loud they could not be ignored. For certain many would have been offended, but God was pleased.

Tabatha was a young lady who was passionate for God. Those around her had no doubt who she stood for. One evening she was at a party where people started to dare each other to do things. Someone dared the girls to lie on top of the boys. Many of the girls were intimidated, they did not want to do it, but felt unable to say no. Tabatha could say no. Immediately she objected, "There is no way I am going to do that."

Because of her stand many of the other girls were able to follow her lead. There, just in her ordinary everyday life, simply by being herself and exhibiting the character of Christ, Tabatha had made a difference. People could choose to disagree with what she did, but her actions were so loud that she could not be ignored.

Clearing up history

Josiah did not restrict himself simply to the desolation caused by the idolatry of his own generation. He looked back to the generations that had gone before him. King Solomon, the son of King David, the wisest king of all time, the last king to preside over a united Israel and the builder of the very temple that King Josiah had cleaned up, was himself drawn into idolatry by the many wives he had married to form political alliances with other kingdoms.

2 Kings 23:13 tells us that King Josiah desecrated the high places that Solomon had set in place. In other words, these idols had remained

in the nation since the days of Solomon and had gone unchallenged by even the godly leaders who preceded Josiah. They had been around for so long that they had become part of the furniture. If there had been a national heritage organisation for Judah, whose job it was to preserve sites of historical significance, then these altars set up by the great King Solomon would surely be considered by the committee. People would have passed them regularly; they would have used them to give directions to others coming into town. And now, overnight, they were gone.

To get an idea of how radical these reforms were, picture the church building where you fellowship. Imagine someone suddenly believes that they've received revelation, backed by Scripture, that the colour blue is sinful. Imagine they take their belief one step further and decide to remove everything blue from the church building and the surrounding area. We're not simply talking about painting over the blue doors, but ripping them off their hinges and totally destroying them. Any books with blue on the cover would not be locked in a cupboard, but burnt in the car park in full view of everyone.

How would you feel if someone was doing this? What if you were the proud owner of a blue Mercedes that had just been towed to the junk yard, with the anti-blue lunatic sitting in the driving seat of the tow-truck? This is how many saw Josiah's reforms. He was not being polite, he was seriously rocking the boat, but he didn't care.

King Josiah had no regard for tradition, for people's opinions or even for his own popularity. His only aim was to please the God of Abraham. The Spirit of God was clearly at work in him, otherwise he would not have had such courage to follow through on his convictions. After all, his father had been murdered because he was an unpopular king and now Josiah was risking angering the idol worshippers in his kingdom to such a degree that they would have enough reason, in their eyes, to remove him from the throne permanently. Some of these idol worshippers had even sacrificed their own children to please their gods. They would not think twice about destroying the king to defend their deities. Josiah was shining a light in a very dark place and he would have made many enemies.

Of course, before we can change the world around us, a revolution usually has to begin inside of us. We can have the world's way of doing things so ingrained in us that we are in no way positioned to bring change. To put it another way, we need to get rid of the idolatrous altars in our own lives before we can deal with the ones around us. The Josiah Generation is not simply a generation who will bring about external reforms, but more importantly they are ones who will deal with the real issues in their own lives to come to a place of radical wholeness. They will truly be those who are "in the world, but not of the world."

One day Tom came to me and asked for some help. He was struggling with his temper. "I get into a fight at school nearly every day and I just can't stop myself. Will you pray for me?" I prayed a very simple prayer with him, that God would help him. Then during the week I continued to pray for him until I knew God had given him the full breakthrough.

The next week Tom came running up to me. He could not wait to speak: "You'll never guess what. I didn't lose my temper once this week!" Something had been broken over his life. The Josiah Generation will not simply move in the power of God and do radical things for His kingdom, they will exhibit the character of Christ.

As God works deep inside members of the Josiah Generation He is preparing them to do great things for His kingdom. He Himself goes on to release them into the ministry of reformation that He has called them to.

Marilyn was six years old. She loved God and had just started to develop a real hunger to hear God's voice. Her leader had been praying for her as usual during the week and had heard that God was calling Marilyn to be an evangelist. The leader simply wrote this down in her prayer journal so that she could pray into it more, but she did not tell anyone what she had heard.

That Sunday Marilyn heard God speaking to her. "God just said He wants me to be an evangelist," she declared.

The leader screamed out, "God told me exactly the same thing earlier this week!"

The whole group were excited that God had spoken the same thing to Marilyn and their leader. It was clear that God was confirming the call on her young life.

In that year Marilyn, age six, led fourteen of her friends to Jesus.

This is the radical edge that God is giving to the Josiah Generation. Just as King Josiah was bold to obey God, so they will be. Josiah had his eyes set on pleasing God. That was his whole goal in life. This does not mean that he did not act as king, judging disputes and overseeing the organisation of the kingdom. But he did not allow such practical duties to pull him away from the spiritual duty that God had given him.

This generation's primary call is to fulfil their duty to God and this will express itself not just through the excellence in which they pursue their earthly duties, but in the way that they bring a vision of God's kingdom on earth into reality.

7

Overstepping Boundaries

"In the cities of Manasseh, Ephraim and Simeon, as far as Naphtali, and in the ruins around them, he tore down the altars and the Asherah poles and crushed the idols to powder and cut to pieces all the incense altars throughout Israel."
(2 Chronicles 34:6-7 paraphrased)

This is not your territory

Andrew, age 12, had invited one of his friends to church. Mohammed was from a Muslim home and he loved his first experience of church. But when he got home he had a shock in store for him. He told his mum all about his experience in church and she beat him because he had gone there.

The next day at school, when Mohammed told Andrew what had happened, Andrew was devastated by what he heard. He called up Mohammed's mum and arranged to go round and talk about it. For over an hour they sat at the table discussing the incident in a very civil and mature way. Andrew shared the gospel with Mohammed's mum and she explained how they were from a different religion, so Mohammed would not be able to convert to Christianity.

After several more discussions in the weeks that followed, however, God brought about a real change. She promised not to beat Mohammed and said she was sorry that she had beaten him for going to church. She even allowed Mohammed to attend the church again, but said he would not be allowed to change his religion as they were Muslims.

At this point Andrew asked his small group leader from church if he would speak to the mum. Again, they had a very long conversation during which she explained that as Muslims they could not change religion. Andrew's leader was able to share the testimony of his own journey from Islam to Christianity and the difference his conversion had made. She was amazed to discover that he had done the impossible and converted from Islam.

When you look at this story it is clear that Andrew had no right or authority to intervene in the discipline that took place at his friend's home. Mohammed's mum did not need to listen to Andrew and was completely within her rights to shield her own son from a different religion.

But Andrew overstepped the natural boundaries that were in place because he saw things as God wanted them to be. His heart for his friend meant that he was willing to ignore the traditional social/ religious boundaries and simply obey the Spirit of God.

The Josiah Generation will have no regard for previous protocols, but will live life according to God's plan. This is the example that King Josiah himself set as he stepped over the boundary of his kingdom into Israel.

To fully understand the revolution that Josiah brought about, we need to take a brief look at the history of Israel to see the context in which he acted. His actions were radical, as is the call on this generation.

A brief history of Israel

Abraham entered into a covenant with God and the nation of Israel had begun. Abraham had one son who fulfilled this covenant, Isaac. Then Isaac had a son, Jacob and Jacob had twelve sons, who became the leaders of the twelve tribes of Israel. One of these sons, Joseph, ended up in Egypt and before long all of Jacob's family had joined him in Egypt. They stayed there for 400 years, by which time they were in slavery, so God sent Moses (and several plagues) to get them out of Egypt.

Once out of Egypt, the Israelites wandered around the desert with Moses until finally, with Joshua as their leader, they entered the Promised Land, kicking out the current residents to set up their permanent home. From the time that they lived in the Promised Land the Judges ruled the land, keeping order and instructing people to keep close to God. But before long, during the time of the final judge, Samuel, the people decided they wanted a king who was more tangible than God to rule over their nation.

So Saul became the first king of Israel ruling over the twelve tribes. He was followed by David, who in turn was followed by his son, Solomon (the wise one, who built the temple in Jerusalem where all of Israel was called to go to worship God). When Solomon died his son, Rehoboam, followed him. But Rehoboam made a big mistake. When the people asked for him to slacken their load a bit and reduce the amount of taxes they had to pay, he promised to be even harsher than his dad. Then, just as God had spoken through His prophets, the kingdom was split into two. Jeroboam stepped up to the plate and became the King of part of Israel and poor Rehoboam was left with just Judah. A bit later on the tribe of Benjamin also joined him.

So Jeroboam, who ruled over the other ten tribes was called the king of Israel, and Rehoboam was just the king of Judah (which included the tribes of Judah and of Benjamin). The city of Jerusalem was situated in the kingdom of Judah. In it was the temple Solomon had built to be the focal point for worship of the God of Israel.

Jeroboam knew that to keep the kingdoms separate and to secure his rule, he had to stop people from going to Jerusalem to worship. Immediately he set up two golden calves, one in the northern part of his kingdom in Dan, and one on the way to Jerusalem at the southern boundary of his kingdom in Bethel. Now he hoped that the people of his kingdom would not go to Jerusalem to worship. For some, the journey to Jerusalem was a long one, so now they could go to Dan. Others were diverted to worship the golden calf in Bethel, without having to cross the boundary into Judah.

So the people of Israel continued with wayward kings for the next couple of hundred years, while the prophets warned them of the consequences. Eventually the Assyrians raided the land and killed many of them, leading others into captivity. Around 100 years before Josiah became the king of Judah, the ten tribes of the kingdom of Israel had been taken into exile. A few people remained in the land, and some of the Assyrians had also taken up residence there.

Then King Josiah, king of Judah came on the scene.

As was prophesied

King Josiah, king of Judah, stepped over the border into the nation of Israel and went straight to the altar of Bethel. This altar was the very symbol of the divided kingdom and, by implication, of the rebellion of God's people against Him. Josiah took the bones of priests and burnt them on the altar at Bethel, desecrating it so that it could never be used again. Its destruction symbolised the fact that the path to the reunification of the nation of Israel was now open. All of Israel was once more permitted to worship God in Jerusalem.

Of course, many others had tried to bring unity to Israel. In the early days of the split, Israel and Judah had been at war with one another, whilst others sought to bring the nation back together as one. It wasn't the right time for reunification to happen. Some had captured the vision of how God wanted things to be, but it was not their destiny to lead the nation there. King Josiah, however, was the one God's people had been waiting for.

In the same way, many have laboured hard to bring about change in the church. The Joshua Generation, for example, have been breaking new ground and preparing new ways, but the Josiah Generation are the ones who are now called to stand up and fulfil the prophesies that have hung over the nations for centuries. They will bring about the change that many have prayed and longed for over many years.

In one secondary school in London, a couple of the Christian teachers had been praying faithfully for years that Jesus would become more central to the school. But any attempts they made seemed to be knocked back. It took the work of some members of the Josiah Generation before true Christian assemblies were established and groups for students to discuss God started to spring up in the school. The vision had been there among the godly for a long time, but it took a special generation to fulfil the vision.

What prophesies do you know of that are still awaiting fulfilment? There has been a growing sense for many that God is preparing a revival that will sweep across Europe. I believe the Josiah Generation will be key players in spearheading this transformation. For when the Spirit of God leads a generation, the will of God is accomplished.

Hey, crazy man, stop

Alex was five years old when he started to tell people about Jesus. His church was holding a special evangelistic concert for children and Alex really wanted his best friend to be there and to get saved. There were three friends in particular that he had been praying for. He really wanted them at the concert so that they could meet his Jesus.

He went to school full of enthusiasm and armed with flyers and tickets for the concert. But, when he was in the middle of handing out the flyers, one of the teachers saw what he was doing and stopped him. Alex had to speak to the head teacher who banned him from inviting anyone in the school to the concert.

But Alex already knew how to pray. Undeterred, he prayed to God that at least one of his friends would come and get saved. He told his cell leader, Toyin, all about it, and she was simply thrilled that he was so full of faith in the face of such opposition. She didn't give it any more thought until the day of the concert.

At the start of the concert Toyin was being her usual friendly self. She got chatting to some parents who did not yet know Jesus and they had a very warm conversation. When their five-year old daughter responded to the gospel appeal, Toyin was there to help her take the first steps of her spiritual life. As they talked about the decision she had made that day, Toyin discovered that it was Alex who had invited her to come. Now Toyin was reaping the fruit of Alex's prayers.

The parents, who felt they had built a rapport with Toyin, were delighted to find out that their daughter's school friend was in Toyin's group and without any hesitation agreed to bring her along to church each Sunday. God had answered Alex's prayers in such a supernatural way. Alex knew that not even the school's head teacher could stop him from doing what God had told him to do.

Alex was an unstoppable five-year old. Even opposition from those in authority over him did not deter him from pursuing his mission from God. He is a part of the Josiah Generation, following in the footsteps of King Josiah.

King Josiah did not just stop at the borders of his kingdom, he continued to pull down altars and idols throughout the land of Israel. His advisors must have been tearing their hair out with concern. This man was going into territory where the Assyrians ruled. Historically it may have belonged to Israel, but now the few Israelites who remained in the land were under the subjection of the Assyrian kingdom.

Yet even this did not deter Josiah. 2 Chronicles 34:6 tell us that he went into the towns of Manasseh, Ephraim and Simeon, even as far as Naphtali, tearing down altars, wreaking havoc and executing the same spiritual purification as he'd done in his own land.

The land for the tribe of Simeon was situated south of the kingdom of Judah. To get to the rest of the kingdom of Israel the Simeonites had to pass through the kingdom of Judah. Many of them had emigrated to Judah and in many ways the tribe was seen as a part of Judah by the time Josiah was king. In fact, their land is not mentioned in the invasion of Assyria into Israel, suggesting that this land could have officially become part of Josiah's legitimate territory.

2 Chronicles 15:9 speaks of a previous time of revival when members of Simeon, Manasseh and Ephraim had all moved into the kingdom of Judah in the time of King Asa. They would have looked to him as king, but they were also living within the boundaries of his kingdom. Those who had moved to Judah had given up their claim to their tribal lands, and these lands had now been taken over and officially belonged to Assyria. Although the king had no authority in these lands, there would have been plenty of people in his kingdom who would have been very sympathetic to his cause, perhaps even hoping that their lands would be restored to them.

Maybe some declared that Josiah was now the king of all Israel, since the king of Israel was now in exile. But even if this was the word on the street, Josiah's leaders and advisors would not have felt so comfortable. After all, those from the tribe of Manasseh and Ephraim had settled a long time ago in their kingdom. Members of the tribes, who had not moved to Judah previously, were now mostly in exile. The king of Assyria had sent people to live in the land from his wider kingdom; it was no longer their land. If they wanted it back they would have to rebel against the Assyrian rule and fight for it. But in spite of this, Josiah did not hesitate to go through their land.

His actions could easily have been seen as a declaration of war against the current incumbents. In removing their places of worship, he was effectively stating that he was more powerful than the gods of the kingdom of Assyria. In removing their gods he was removing the supposed source of their power and potentially provoking them to fight.

Not only did Josiah risk war from the outside, he also risked prompting a civil war within his own nation. For the worshippers of other gods, who had already lost their own temples of worship, could have used this opportunity to declare that not only had Josiah brought religious instability (from their point of view), but he was now also bringing political instability. They could have stirred up the crowds, showing that for years the different religions had lived peacefully side by side, but now Josiah was bringing disunity. Yet, Josiah smashed through the boundaries of current convention without fear, and with divine favour.

Beyond comfortable boundaries

On one mission we took a young girl called Leona with us. Whilst we had been praying for the mission, she had heard from God that she was to deliver a letter to a lady wearing black clothing who had black hair and black eye shadow. She had seen a clear picture of this lady and to us it sounded like a Goth. The likelihood of finding someone dressed this way in a market town of middle England seemed pretty small to me, but I have learnt not to comment on these things and just wait to see what happens. She wrote a letter to the lady as God had instructed her and was all set to go.

On the day of the mission we arrived in the market town and started walking around. There, right in the middle of the town, stood a gothic group. And there, at the very centre of the group, stood the exact lady that Leona had seen in her vision. Many children perceive an invisible boundary between themselves and members of the Goth subculture, but Leona stepped over that boundary and went to deliver the letter.

The lady opened the letter and read the first line: "I am writing this letter to save you." We stayed in that town for several more hours, walking around looking for other people. Every time we passed the town centre we saw the same group of people standing around. They would smile at Leona each time she passed them and, more significantly, for the whole time we were there, every member of our team noticed that the letter Leona had written was being passed around as each one of the Goths read and re-read what she had written.

Just like King Josiah, Leona had crossed over conventional boundaries to obey God, without fear of the potential repercussions.

Josiah's reforms even went beyond what we have described so far. He went further still from his earthly kingdom. He stepped right out of his comfort zone. The next focal point for Josiah's crusade against false worship took him as far as Naphtali. There is no mention of the inhabitants of Naphtali ever living in the kingdom of Judah. The land of Naphtali was about as far from Judah as you could get.

Naphtali practically encompassed the tribe of Dan at the most northern part of Israel, where there had always been a close allegiance between the two. Some even suggest that the two had become as one. The second golden calf, that had been set up when the kingdom split, was located in Dan and it too would have been destroyed.

King Josiah was now in a territory where the only way he could claim to be allowed there would be by appealing to history. He had to look back and declare that a united Israel was not only a fact from the past, but also God's desire for the future. In political terms this was not an argument that would hold water. But Josiah pressed on with his task regardless and somehow he got away with it too.

As if the writer in 2 Chronicles had not made it clear enough, he concludes by adding that King Josiah worked his transformation "throughout all Israel".

Josiah was totally reckless for the cause. He was perfectly happy to rock his world and those around him if it meant that he was fulfilling the call of God. In the same way, the Josiah Generation will not be concerned about political correctness or protocols.

Instead they will be concerned with getting the job done!

King Josiah sought to destroy altars where sacrifices were made to false gods. He assaulted Asherah poles where scenes of immorality took place in the name of worship. He crushed idols to powder and, in so doing, demonstrated their complete lack of power. Let's not forget that some of this false worship had been in the kingdom for centuries – it had been a part of the fabric of society beyond anyone's living memory.

Not only that, but other altars would have been added far more recently as the Assyrians relocated in the land, bringing their own gods with them. Once more Josiah was providing a direct challenge to the occupying forces.

The Assyrians themselves were not ignorant concerning the God of Israel. Soon after they moved into the land many of them had been killed by a plague of lions that God sent. Because of this, some of the priests of Israel had been brought back into the land, to ensure that the God of the land of Israel continued to be worshipped alongside their own gods. But now Josiah was stating that throughout the land, the worship of the God of Israel was to be the only worship allowed. Josiah, king of Judah, did not rest until he had completely transformed the landscape of the whole of the nation of Israel.

Compared to the standards of the day, this crusade was not enacted through violence against people. A few priests lost their lives in the process, but there was not a significant death toll. However, by striking at the heart of people's religions it was an aggressive assault. This no-compromise attitude would have set everybody talking and stirred some to action.

The Josiah Generation will share this no-compromise attitude, not seeking to gain popularity or, indeed, to deliberately offend those around them, but simply seeking to please God and only God. This generation will bring reforms across denominational divides and, in the face of historical challenges, extend their influence to the very fringes of church society, touching nominal Christians and Christian institutions alike. In short, they will be God's agents to help bring about a radical change to the church that will result in the church being what God has called it to be.

There is a traditional children's story called "The Emperor's New Clothes". It tells of an emperor who was conned by weavers into wearing a robe which they said was woven with material that could only be seen by those who were not stupid, unfit for their position or incompetent. When the emperor paraded in these new (non-existent) clothes, everyone could see immediately that he was naked, but nobody dared speak out for fear that they too would be shown up as being stupid. It took a child to speak out about the Emperor's nakedness before change could take place.

This is part of the call on the Josiah Generation as they talk about things as they really are. The deeper they study God's Word, the more they will gladly point out our inconsistencies. The Josiah Generation will bring many pearls of wisdom to the church as they speak out what some have been thinking, but have not voiced. This in turn will act as a catalyst for change.

The Josiah Generation will not know any boundaries or restrictions on them as they pursue the call of God for their lives. We have seen some of the ways that God is already using the Josiah Generation while they are children. How much more will they be able to do as they grow into maturity? As we continue to train this generation in the way they should go, when they reach maturity they will accomplish great things for God's kingdom.

8
Rebuilding
The Temple

"In the eighteenth year of [Josiah's] *reign, when he had purged the land and the temple, he sent Shaphan the son of Azaliah, Maaseiah the governor of the city, and Joah the son of Joahaz the recorder, to repair the house of the LORD his God."*

(2 Chronicles 34:8)

Glory from the ruins

Jonathan had been in the church for many years. He came along to the various programmes ,but he was unhappy in himself. He had had to face many issues as he was growing up and, although he was still attending church, it was clear at the age of 13 that he only showed up out of duty. His physical presence was there, but the rest of him stayed home in bed each week.

Jonathan started to hang out with a rougher crowd as he sought to find his identity and get the affirmation he craved. His new friends welcomed him into the fold and his life was set on a dark path. He started to rap, and the language of gang culture infiltrated all his lyrics. The attitude of the culture invaded his life. Things were going from bad to worse until he was caught in possession of a sawn-off shot gun.

Jonathan was placed in a young offenders' institution for several weeks while the case against him was prepared for trial in the courts. Things did not look favourable for him. The reality of it all was beginning to sink in.

All who came into contact with Jonathan in the institution saw that there was something different about him. His Christian roots were still evident. To the staff who worked there it was clear that he was like a fish out of water in that environment. But the choices he'd made had consequences.

During this whole time his parents and the church kept him in prayer and visited him to chat to him along the way. The standard questions were asked of how one raised in the church could go so far from his purpose. The prison chaplain also kept a special eye out for him.

Finally, the case was brought before a judge. From the opening moments in the court room it was clear that this crime was to be taken very seriously. On the back of a wave of violent crime among young people in the city, the judicial system was being presented with an opportunity to send out a message to the youth of the community that this kind of crime will be dealt with severely. Here was an opportunity to make an example out of Jonathan. The whole case was heading towards him being locked away for a long time.

In the middle of the hearing the fire alarm went off in the building. The court was suspended and we all gathered outside the building. During this "extra" time Jonathan's solicitor was able to develop the counterarguments needed to prevent him from going to prison.

The judge conceded that, though he wanted to lock Jonathan away, there was a legal precedent preventing this, since it was his first time before the court. Instead, Jonathan received various legal orders and was given hours of community service to complete. He left with a stern warning of no mercy should he return to the court on any further offence.

Once out of jail, Jonathan met the Lord for himself. He became a changed man. He continued his rapping, but the language changed from gang culture to God-culture. His whole demeanour changed and with it, those around him started to look up to him.

He still faced struggles along the way, but now he knew God was with him, so he was always able to find a way through the struggles. He became a clear role model for his peers. Jonathan, raised in the church, became church to those around him.

This kind of dramatic change in Jonathan's landscape is similar to what took place under King Josiah. The young king had been brought up in a place where the God of the Jews was declared Lord, but given no room in everyday life. The temple still stood, but it had been desecrated by false gods and had been so neglected that it was now in a state of disrepair. The local priests had deserted their posts, with some even becoming priests for other religions. What should have been the throne room from which the presence of God was visible to the whole earth, was instead a place where God was mocked.

King Josiah had already evicted the altars to false gods from the temple, but there was still much repair work to be done. Not only did the building need repairing, but the priests also needed to be called back to their original jobs.

The desertion of the priests could not be blamed entirely on them. For certain, some individuals had chosen to follow foreign gods and only had themselves to blame for their own sin. Many however, would simply have been unable to survive as priests in a nation that had backslidden so far from God's plans. Priests were dependent on the whole population bringing their tithes and offerings, from which they were allowed to take some as food, while they devoted their time to serving the Lord. If no offerings were brought, then there would be no food for the priests. They would have had little alternative but to seek employment elsewhere. The paucity of the priests was a reflection of the whole of society under the previous kings of Judah. With a weaker priesthood this in turn would lead to even less people following the true God as He slipped from the mainstream of society to be observed by the few.

In the same way, where there is weakness among the adult church, the next generation suffer. Where the worship of God is no longer a central part of the church, children are being kept from His presence. In some churches the worship for the adults is strong, but the children are left to sit to one side or simply sing cute songs rather than engaging with God.

For the priests in the temple it was time for them to stop playing church and to start being the church, fulfilling their priestly duties. God had ordained this season to be one where the priesthood would be restored. This same mandate is on the Josiah Generation.

As I have worked with children in different settings I have often seen this shift take place as the altar of God is repaired among the young. They are called back to their destiny as priests before God. They then start to rise as worshippers of God.

One group of teenage boys that I was leading had become very self-conscious about singing out loud to God. The worship times we held together were beginning to weaken. Over time, I started to call them back to worshipping God. The breakthrough came after we took some of them away to get their hearts right with God again.

One week, as we started to worship, one of the boys just took off in worship. He no longer cared about what others thought, he was just singing his heart out to God. Once the group had got over the shock of this initial change, they caught up with him and for over an hour they poured out their hearts in worship to God while I stood back and marvelled at what He was doing.

That one boy was Jonathan – the same Jonathan who a few months back had been facing jail. A transformation had taken place in him and he was now influencing others.

Following the template

Josiah's plan was to restore the temple, repairing the structure along the way. From the Scriptures he could determine how it should be. A love for God goes hand in hand with a love for the Scriptures.

When our eldest son Joshua was born we had many words spoken over his life that he would be prophetic. During the first couple of weeks of his life he struggled to breast feed and had to be fed in part by bottle. A few weeks in, both he and mum were getting the hang of feeding. One day, as we were driving along in our car, I felt God saying to me that this was a prophetic word.

Of course, I ignored it, assuming that my imagination had led me to believe that anything my child did had prophetic significance. But the nudge of the Spirit continued, so I tuned into God and listened as He told me that this was a prophetic word for his church worldwide.

"For years people have been dependant on preachers to give them the Word, but I am calling my church to feed from me directly."

Of course, formula milk is a good simulation of breast milk, but it is not perfect. It does not contain the same level of protection against diseases, nor is there the same intimacy in feeding. God is calling each member of His church to study the Word for themselves.

For the Josiah Generation this is a key part of their calling, for if they are to rebuild the temple in their day then they need to know what it is supposed to look like.

Often people's Bible knowledge does not grow significantly beyond what they learn in childhood, but we have a responsibility to ensure that children not only know the Scriptures, but they have a desire to keep on learning from them.

To the average child the Bible can seem boring if it is not applied to their lives. But when children read something in the Bible, try it out in their school, and discover what a difference it makes, then it suddenly becomes a living book. As they live out the promises of God and gain the benefits, they start to become excited to discover what else is in the Bible for them.

If each day they are encouraged to spend time reading the Bible, then they will grow as individuals in God's kingdom. Their foundation will be secure and the risk of them being sidetracked by a minor doctrine, or indeed a heretical one, will be significantly reduced. They need to know God's Word to be able to do what He is calling them to do.

It s not just for you

As King Josiah brought these reforms he was not just doing it for his own sake. He was doing it as the leader of Judah and as one called by God. The changes he brought to the temple were central to his drive to reform – not simply to stop people worshipping false gods, but to bring them back to worshipping the one true God. Josiah's work in restoring the temple building, which on the surface looks very practical, was fundamentally founded on spiritual motives. He renewed the covenant between God and His people, calling all people to live according to the divine standard.

For the duration of his reign Josiah's reforms stood strong as he acted as the guardian and influencer of the worship life of the temple. Out of his own pocket he ensured that the sacrifices could be made, and others across all Israel followed his example, ensuring that the priests could fulfil their duties. In fulfilling their duty, the people were reminded regularly to fulfil their own duty in serving the Lord. A single leader had brought about real change in his whole generation.

In one gathering of children that we held, we were celebrating with those who had a birthday that month. Sophia came and joined me on the platform as she had just turned nine. Sophia was a real live wire for the Lord and served Him enthusiastically, whatever she was doing. I knew that she was busy in her school discipling some of her friends, so while she was next to me I asked her to tell us about her work in the school. She told of how she had led four of her friends to Jesus and was meeting with them regularly, to help them grow more with Him.

One of these friends was there at that meeting, so I called her up on to the platform as well to share her side of the story. This beautiful girl, wearing a top with the word Pineapple written across it, came to stand next to me. She was the same age as Sophia and I couldn't help but call her "Pineapple" – a nickname that has stuck in my head ever since. Pineapple told of how Sophia had shared with her about Jesus, how she had chosen to follow Jesus for herself, and how she now met weekly with Sophia to learn more. She also told of how she had come along on a Sunday from time to time and really enjoyed it.

The following weekend we were planning a special day away for children to encounter God for themselves. The thought popped into my mind that it would be great for Pineapple to be there with us. So there on the platform I started to tell her about the day away and I had planned in my mind to pay for her place if she could come.

As it turned out I didn't need to. Not only was Pineapple already booked to come on the day, but so were the other three members of Sophia's group. Sophia had already spoken to them about it and got their parents' permission for them to join us. So instead I ended up inviting Sophia to come along as their leader.

On that day God really showed up and all of Sophia's friends met with God in a very special way. The change was so noticeable that a couple of weeks later, Pineapple's mum came to church and responded to the gospel for herself.

Just as Josiah spearheaded change and then influenced others to bring change as well, so the nature of the Josiah Generation is to bring about change in those around them, who in turn will influence others, so that the society at large will be touched and true worship will be restored to God.

A group of young people, who all attended the same school, decided that they wanted to give out Bibles to every person in their school.

They came to their church to ask for the money to be able to do this. The church considered the proposal, but before they could even give an answer, the teenagers found funding from elsewhere and were able to give Bibles to all the pupils!

You are not alone

When it came to restoring the temple, there was no way that King Josiah could have done it all by himself. He may have been the driving force for the destruction of the idols, but it required a move of God among the whole people to enable the true restoration of the temple.

2 Kings 23:2 tells us that when King Josiah went up to the temple to initiate its restoration, "everyone" went with him – priests and prophets, the people of Judah and all those living in Jerusalem, the least and the greatest all went up together. People from all across Israel paid for the temple to be restored. This was a huge community project and everyone was involved in some way. A characteristic of every revival is a spirit of unity, where people work together for the good of the kingdom and King Josiah's time was no exception.

The Josiah Generation are not called to be soloists playing by themselves in the kingdom of God, rather they are called to work together, creating a symphony of revival that will be audible in the world around them. After all, church is not about a few individuals serving God with all their heart, church is about a whole spiritual nation rising up together. If one part of the body is weak, the whole body suffers.

Doing what you are called to do

When it came to restoring the temple there were many jobs that needed to be done. Carpenters and stone masons, equipped not just with the tools for the job, but with all the skills needed, came forward to work on the temple. King Josiah had trustworthy people around him and they in turn were able to appoint others to oversee and administer this huge project.

Each person involved had their own unique mix of giftings and each one could use them to help with the temple. They were created for this time and ready to fulfil their call. It was almost as if each one had received their own personal call from God. In the same way that King Josiah had been prepared for his role from birth, so had those around him.

A whole army of obedient soldiers is being raised up in this next generation who are not only swift to obey God's call, but have the unique giftings needed to do it. The only thing that remains is for these giftings to be developed, so that they will be ready when their time comes.

This is not simply a movement where spiritual giftings are exercised within the context of a church meeting, in a setting detached from the real world – this is God demonstrating His restoration through the natural. As Sophia led people to Jesus and encouraged them as they followed Him, the effect on their lives was as tangible as the restoration work of the physical temple would have been in the time of King Josiah.

Under the Josiah Generation the church will break out in new ways to bring real change to the world around them.

John is a great example of this. One day he was stood waiting for a London underground train to arrive at Earls Court tube station. As he waited for the train, he heard the Holy Spirit speak to him and instruct him to go to a different platform. His train was still quite a few minutes off, but it was a good five minute walk within the station to get to the other platform.

John obeyed and, as he stepped onto the other platform, he saw a girl from his school that he had been praying for over the past few weeks. They got chatting and he had just enough time to lead her to Jesus before her train arrived. Sprinting back to his platform, he arrived just in time to step onto his own train. His act of obedience

– and indeed the immediacy with which he acted – resulted in one more soul being added to the kingdom.

The Josiah Generation will shine out brightly in this world. We know that not everything will be perfect, but wherever this generation go they will make a difference for God. The church is breaking out. We have a privileged opportunity to help prepare the next generation to be part of this move of God.

9

A Blueprint For The Future

"However there need be no accounting made with them of the money delivered into their hand, because they deal faithfully."
(2 Kings 22:7)

Crazy For God

What drove King Josiah to such levels of craziness? What zeal had caught hold of him that made him so reckless in his pursuit of God's plan? Nothing short of a blueprint from heaven for how God intended things to be and a revelation of the divine vision for Israel could have enabled him to carry out the task.

God did not intend for Israel to be a divided nation, He desired His nation to be whole. Though it had split due to the idolatry of Solomon and the disobedience of the people, this was not God's plan. The kingdom was supposed to be one and Josiah was acting as if that intention was already a reality.

To put it another way, Josiah had faith to believe that the things that were not, would be. He was sure of what he hoped for and certain of what he did not see. God had given him what he needed to fulfil the task. Josiah's actions took a significant step towards the reunification, something that would later be built on when the nation of Judah would itself be in exile in a few generation's time.

When things work as they should it can be surprising to us today, but in the season of the Josiah Generation they will live as if things are as they should be, with the sure knowledge that one day they will be.

Joash was eight years old. He had led many of his friends to the Lord and met with them regularly at school to teach them about Jesus and encourage them to live for Him. One day Joash had to go into hospital for an investigation. His friends saw that he was not in school that day. When they heard that he was in hospital they got together and prayed for him. No one had told them what to do, but Joash had been equipping them to live for Jesus. This is just the way that it should be – they were living according to the blueprint of church.

No Account Required

Mark had just turned eight. He loved his school, he loved his friends, but most of all he loved and lived for Jesus. He had been speaking to his friend Andy about Jesus for a while, but this week was special. It was this week when Andy chose to follow Jesus and Mark was the one who was able to lead him in a prayer of salvation. With this new bond of trust between them, Andy shared his greatest secret that had weighed him down for years.

When Andy was at home he was regularly accused of stealing money from him mum's purse. In fact, he did not do it, but the facts were stacked up against him. Money was going missing from her purse and the money was appearing in his money box. He protested each time he was "caught", but with the facts so clearly before them, his parents were not going to be taken in by his stories.

Andy shared with Mark how he never took any money from his mum, but instead it was his older brother who sometimes stole the money and planted it for safe keeping in Mark's money box to be retrieved later if its absence was not noticed. Mark knew exactly what to do and took the matter straight to the authorities – that is, the highest authority he knew of, God. Together Mark and Andy spoke to God about the issue and asked Him to step in and sort it out.

The next day Andy was relaxing downstairs at home. His mum had just spotted that more money was missing and was marching up to his room to find it. As she entered his room she had a shock. There, in Andy's room, was his older brother placing the money into Andy's money box. He had been caught red handed. Mum remembered all the times that Andy had protested his innocence and blamed his brother in the past. She knew now he had been telling the truth all along.

That evening both his parents spoke to Andy and asked him to forgive them. Within twenty-four hours of Andy following Christ, his greatest challenge in life had been removed.

Of course, not everything turns out so miraculously, as anyone who has been a believer for longer than a few months will testify, but this is still the blueprint that we are to work to, trusting that God will fill in the gaps. The apostle Paul underwent persecution and imprisonment, but he still saw God's hand in it all. Even when people were preaching the gospel out of spite for him, he still put it down to God being at work.

King Josiah had this same trust in God to oversee the details of the building of the temple. He was willing for the workers to be given the money that had been raised to restore the temple and he trusted them to do it. These workers did not have to give any account to him as to how the money was spent, they were simply trusted. This was the new order of the kingdom.

This is the way it should always be for those who are living honourably before the Lord. But for many of us, used to our health and safety conscious, accountability-crazy, litigation-driven world, this will seem shocking because we have seen too many things go wrong in the past. The "but, what ifs" are at the forefront of our minds. This is because we have become used to the fallen order of the world. The Josiah Generation will be focusing on God's order – the order of how things should be.

When God is central, He deals with issues that are not in line with His purposes. Ananias and Saphira found this out pretty quickly when they tried to lie to the Holy Spirit. The land they sold was theirs and they were free to keep all the money from it, but they acted as if they had given it all away. When they were struck down dead, a message went through the church not to mess with God. But it also sent out a message to the world: this group of people was set apart, different from your normal organisation and to be joined at your own risk!

In fact, if God's manifest presence is evident among His people then sin cannot stay hidden for long. Discernment is sharpened and God's people are sensitive to God's voice. God protects His church. Remember God is a jealous God; He is more keen to guard the reputation of His church than we are. He is just waiting for a people to rise up who are willing to live by His standards again.

With the Josiah generation comes a restoration of standards.

Back to the Designer's template

King Josiah's blueprint was to look back to the original template of a united kingdom. This is what drove him to act as though the kingdom was already reunited, ignoring the perilous state he was potentially putting his kingdom into. He did not care for his own kingdom, he was concerned for God's kingdom. This is what drove him to act as if those around him were trustworthy, since this was the expectation within that kingdom. Josiah knew how things should be and, like a master builder, he was working to the architect's design.

He called people to do what they should have been doing all along and to do it as if this were the norm – because it is the norm for those who are living for God. Anything less is a deviation from God's call. In his lifetime the environment changed from one where the godly were seen as the outsiders of society, to one where the ungodly became the outsiders. The blueprint of the kingdom was being fulfilled.

In the church, we too have a blueprint to work towards. A starting point for the blueprint is the way in which the early church conducted itself and the people grew and related to each other. Many people call for us to return to the model of the early church. But even the state of the early church is not the end point. After all, Paul's letters are full of corrections to the early church and encouragements to help them to keep their focus.

The early church was simply the church in its infancy. It was the baby church that had just been birthed. That we are encouraged to look back to our infancy tells us how much work there is to be done in seeing today's church restored. Instead of looking back to the early church, we should be looking forward to the end time church. The blueprint we should be working to is not that of the new church, but rather that of the mature church which Jesus will return for.

The blueprint for the modern church is in fact the bride of Christ. Jesus' whole return is dependent on the bride rising up, pure and spotless. It is this blueprint to which the Josiah Generation will be working.

This blueprint is something that will be written deep within the lives of this generation.

One day we were having a time of ministry for children from a local estate, focusing especially on bullying. On one side we invited any children who were being bullied to come forward for prayer, on the other side we invited any bullies to come forward who wanted God to help them stop bullying.

Jade was being bullied by Mark. They were both only eight, but Jade's life was becoming unbearable. She hated school because of this one child. Quickly she responded to the offer for prayer. Meanwhile, on the other side of the room Mark had gone forward for prayer. He was desperately unhappy himself and no longer wanted to be a bully.

That Friday was Jade's birthday. That Friday the bullying stopped and she and Mark became good friends. Something of God was written deeply inside both of them. They both continued to attend our outreach programme and you could tell that God was up to something in both their lives.

A few months later one of the playground supervisors, who was a friend of one of the outreach team, told us of something that had taken place that week during break. Jade and Mark had decided to mimic the outreach programme we ran. Mark pretended to be me, while Jade was my co-leader. Several classes of children gathered round to watch as they chose to tell a story. Actually, they didn't just choose any story, they chose the story of the crucifixion. And they didn't just tell the story, they acted it out.

Involving all the children who were around in different parts, they had the wailing women, the soldiers, the robbers on either side, the Pharisees, the man who had to help carry the cross and so on. Not one detail was missing as they choreographed a production with fifty children that I would never have dared attempt even with months of rehearsal. Not only did they act it out, but through it all they brought out the key message of salvation.

Incredibly, we had never trained them for this. Nor had we ever told them the majority of the details they included in the story. We checked with their parents (one of whom had never been to church in her life) to see if they had taught them anything, read the Bible with them, or shown them a DVD. Nothing. God had put the blueprint for salvation deep inside them, so that at the right opportunity, with the help of the Holy Spirit, they simply had to let it out.

This Josiah Generation will understand the centrality of the cross – the foundation from which our entire faith flows – and this will be the platform from which they will long for the return of Christ. For the death and resurrection of Jesus is the source from which our faith flows and the return of Jesus is where our faith is flowing to. Put another way: the cross is our foundation and being the bride is our destination.

God is still in the equation

This focus on Christ's return, seen through the light of His death and resurrection, is a radical shift for many sectors of the church. But if God is instigating it, then God has the details worked out. After all, this is something that has to happen at some point in church history if the bride of Christ is to be fully prepared. I believe that time is now.

If the church were now the pure and spotless bride, many of our current worries concerning the running of church would be irrelevant. If God is still in the equation we don't need to worry about whether someone is dipping their hands into the offering, because God will either expose that person or deal with them directly. Our sole concern should therefore become whether or not we are walking ever closer to God. If our hearts move away from the Father's heartbeat, then aspects of the ministry where He has placed us will start to deteriorate. But when our hearts are close to Him, even if everything around us crumbles, we know that God is working in it all to bring about His bigger purpose: the development of the bride of Christ.

This yearning for the return of Jesus is a key element found in the end time church. As the Josiah Generation start to restore standards and seek to live according to this divine blueprint, they will increasingly yearn for His return and centre their whole lives around this expectation, living as if that day is today. Is this not the warning that Jesus provides in many of the parables about the kingdom of God? We do not know the exact day when Jesus will come back, but we know that He is coming and that we should be ready, expectant of His imminent arrival.

This does not mean that we live our lives blind to the needs of tomorrow. We still need to go to work and earn a living, our children still need to go to school and be educated, and the poor still need to be cared for. We are to live as if Jesus is returning tomorrow, but we are also to live in a way that means we are prepared for life here on earth if He does not come for a month, a decade or longer. We are still to live in this world, even though we are not of it.

Josiah lived and ruled over an earthly kingdom. This kingdom did not fall apart because of the spiritual quest he was on. Instead he fulfilled his duties as king, whilst at the same time obeying his mandate as a follower of God.

As ones who come before the Josiah Generation, we can either help prepare them for this call or we can carry on with business as usual. They will benefit greatly from our help, but even if we fail, God will still be at work to prepare His bride.

The Josiah Generation will live according to the divine blueprint either because of, or in spite of, what they see around them. Either way, God has called this generation to a level of faithfulness in serving Him, so that in the last days they will be able to continue to stand for Him.

As the Josiah Generation learn about the bride of Christ, and fall more in love with God, they will be hastening the days of Jesus' return to earth. The bride prepares herself for the day of marriage, so this generation will be getting ready for their future.

10

Honouring Past Generations

"Then he said, 'What gravestone is this that I see?' So the men of the city told him, 'It is the tomb of the man of God who came from Judah and proclaimed these things which you have done against the altar of Bethel.' And he said, 'Let him alone; let no one move his bones.' So they let his bones alone, with the bones of the prophet who came from Samaria."

(2 Kings 23:17-18)

Radical Roots

Selina had been working hard in her school to lead many of her friends to Jesus and to meet with them regularly. She had a group of around fifteen teenagers who met with her each week and a Christian teacher even popped in to sit with the group and see what God was doing.

Yet Selina wanted something more for her friends.

She remembered the years of training and support she had received from her cell leader and asked if her cell leader could come into the school to minister to her group.

The school gave all the clearance that was needed and so it was with great excitement that the cell leader was able to turn up and share a word with the group. She then went on to pray with them and God clearly touched each one of them. Selina took great encouragement from this as she saw how God could use her more.

As the Josiah Generation works towards the blueprint of the bride of Christ, this does not mean that they will ignore their roots. Nor will they be a generation steeped in arrogance concerning their own call. Such pride would exclude the generations who have gone before them. Rather, they will understand that they are building on the foundations built by previous generations.

The church of Jesus has always been radical. A radical generation understands that it is building on this radical foundation. The apostles are described as those who turned the world upside down with their teachings. The history of the church is a key part of the destiny of the church, as God has been at work preparing His church for the last days.

Josiah sees history

When King Josiah was busy sorting out the wider nation of Israel, one of his key acts was to destroy the altar that King Jeroboam had built in Bethel. Hundreds of years before, Jeroboam had built the altar to stop the Israelites moving into Judah to worship God at Jerusalem. When he had built the altar a prophet, whom the Bible calls "the Man of God," came with a message from God. He announced that God would raise up a man called Josiah who would take the priests who made sacrifices on this altar and sacrifice them on it, burning human bones and thus desecrating the altar. He went on to say, to prove this word was from God, that the altar would split open and the ashes on it would be poured out.

Jeroboam was pretty annoyed at this interruption to his dedication ceremony at the altar. He stretched out his hand to command his soldiers to seize the man of God. But, as he stretched out his hand it shrivelled up and the altar was split open just as the man of God had said.

Hundreds of years later, Josiah was busy being the fulfilment of this prophecy without even realising it. As he was fishing around for dead bones to scatter, he came across a tomb. When he asked who it belonged to, those around him told him of the man of God who had prophesied all those years ago that a man called Josiah would come and destroy the altar exactly as Josiah had just done. The king ordered that the bones of the man, whose prophetic words he was now fulfilling, should be left alone.

Josiah could have just taken the bones, like he had done with the others, and scattered them around. It seems he hadn't heard of the prophecy until the locals told him about it. The mandate he had been following was to obey God, not to fulfil the prophecy of the man of God. Yet when he heard about it, he honoured the man of God from the past.

Josiah was radical, but he was not moving under his own steam, he was moving under the influence of the Spirit of God. His obedience to God was demonstrated in his fulfilment of the prophetic word that had been spoken.

Humility

An important aspect of humility is the ability to recognise how those who have gone before us have helped us to achieve what we are achieving now. Our predecessors are recognised and honoured for their part in our present and future.

Drusilla was a typical teenager whom God had given a double dose of bubble when he created her personality. One day she was on her way to school as usual. As she sat on the bus next to her friend, a man came up to them and told them about Jesus. He put a Bible tract in their hand and walked off. Drusilla's friend was deeply touched by the man's words and the tract he had given her. By the time they got to school, Drusilla had led her friend to the Lord.

Her friend was in tears, visibly moved, so it didn't take long for several other friends to gather round and find out what the matter was. Through the tears the tract was passed around. It was read and re-read, until by break time Drusilla had led eight of her friends to the Lord and spoken to many other people about Jesus.

She had been speaking to them all about Jesus for months, but it took a man older than her to be the catalyst for the mini-revival that took place that day. She could not have done it without him.

In general children find it easier than adults to be humble. Most tend to be well aware of their ignorance of life and their dependence upon others. It is rare to find a child full of pride, and even if you do come across such a child, they are usually easily encouraged onto a path of humility. Indeed, many a child who has been used by God has looked to us for further guidance and encouragement and has thanked their leaders for everything that has been given to them, knowing that they needed that support.

What is harder is for them to remain humble when they grow into adulthood. As God uses them powerfully they will need to remember that it is *God* who is using them – this is not something they can do on their own. By honouring the past generations they will be reminded that they are simply links in a chain, leading to the fulfilment of God's plans on earth.

The Josiah Generation will be working in a time when God is pouring out His blessing as the church is growing in unity – unlike many previous generals in God's kingdom, who fought and sacrificed as lone voices in spiritual deserts during their time to bring the church to the place where it is today.

Humility will keep their focus on the fact that they are simply servants of God. When a servant does what his master tells him to, there is no great reward in store for that servant – he is simply doing what is expected of him. Others may marvel at what the servant is doing and how God is using him, but for him, he is simply obeying the call of God.

This will be the attitude of the Josiah Generation. There is no "Plan B" for their lives. They are simply doing what they should be doing. This is not a cause for celebration, indeed the surprise would be if they weren't doing it. Such a paradigm shift in thinking will happen because of the focus that this generation will have on being the bride of Christ. Through understanding their past they will be propelled towards their future, working towards the blueprint that God has set for them.

11
The Heart of God

"Thus it happened, when the king heard the words of the Law, that he tore his clothes."

(2 Chronicles 34:19)

God knows each person

God knows each and every person. This was brought home to me in a very real way when we took some of our young people out onto the streets to share about Jesus. Before we went, everyone had prayed and heard from God regarding who He wanted them to speak to on the streets.

One girl heard God telling her about a lady called Fiona. Fiona, God told her, had been in a car accident, was stressed out and on drugs. The girl also saw a picture of Fiona, a red-haired lady wearing stylish clothes. She wrote a letter to Fiona telling her how much God loves her.

When we went out onto the streets, we met someone who was

wearing exactly the same clothes as the girl had seen in her vision. Indeed, every detail about her was identical to what this girl had seen when praying, except that her hair was brown.

Undeterred the girl, with a friend, went up to the lady and asked, "Excuse me, but is your name Fiona?"

The lady looked startled and a bit puzzled.

"Well my middle name is Fiona," she replied hesitantly.

Encouraged by this first response, the girl continued with more boldness:

"Have you been in a car accident?"

"I was in an accident a year ago."

"Are you on drugs?"

At this Fiona laughed.

"No, I don't take drugs, but I am still on medication because of the car accident!"

With all this confirmation the girl was sure she had found the person who God had spoken to her about. She handed over the letter she had written, explaining that God had told her to write this. Fiona opened the letter and as she read it through, tears filled her eyes. She was having her own personal encounter with God in the middle of the high street.

But one thing was still bugging the girl.

"God showed me that you had red hair, but your hair is not red. How come?"

"My natural hair colour is red, but I have dyed it brown."

God knew and loved Fiona, a random lady on the street. He knew her middle name and her original hair colour. He knew she had been in a car crash and was still on medication. He knew she was stressed and needing Him. Not only that, but He knew three weeks in advance what clothes she would choose to wear on that day and that she would be shopping in the same town where we were going to be. Even though at this stage Fiona didn't know God, God knew her and cared for her.

God knows the details of every one of the six billion plus people on planet earth. As the Bible says, even the hairs on our head are numbered (and the original colour known).

Anyone tapping into God will quickly start to develop His heart for people. After all, it was God's love for people that sent Him looking for Adam in the Garden of Eden after he and Eve had sinned. It was God's love that rescued the Israelites from slavery and ultimately God's love that caused Him to come into this world to die for our sins on a cross. God is love. He quite simply oozes love and those who know Him increasingly do the same.

It is possible to be so radical for a cause that you miss the very people that the cause is intended to help. It is easy, in being cutthroat with sin, to deal harshly with the people who God loves so dearly. Yet King Josiah, with all his zeal in destroying idols and casting judgment on the priests, still managed to remain tender hearted.

The tearing of the robes

King Josiah had ordered the temple to be restored and had given the money to the workmen, trusting them to complete the task. In the process of carrying out this restoration they came across the book of the law. This book was taken straight to the king and read before him. He had clearly not heard its contents before, for as he heard it something broke inside of him.

Overcome with grief for his sins and the sins of his people, he tore his robe, for he knew what they deserved from God. The tearing of clothes in Bible days was a sign of overwhelming grief. Nowadays we would describe our hearts as being cut to pieces – in those days people wore their hearts on their sleeves and literally tore their clothing to pieces. When King Josiah tore his robe he was showing the state of his heart and was humbling himself before God. With his royal robes torn, he was demonstrating his desire that God would once more be King of the nation.

Josiah's heart for the people in all of his actions is evident. He was not simply a man on a crusade, he was a man who saw why his people were suffering and in danger of exile and recognised that the only solution was for them to come back to God.

At this stage in his reign he had already done much damage to the idols around him, yet he did not rest on his laurels. He knew that he and his people needed God's mercy to survive this crisis. Josiah's whole life was one of sacrificing his own personal comfort for the benefit of those whom he was leading. The Josiah Generation will share that same heart of compassion for those around them.

One day we took some of our children out onto the streets just to share God's love with people. Each group thought about what they wanted to do, prepared for all the work, and then arrived early on Sunday ready to show the love of God to people.

As one group gave out sweets to those passing by, an old Muslim lady was sitting by herself at a bus stop. One of the children left the group to go to her and offer her a sweet. The lady was so touched by this simple expression of love that she gave the child a hug and kissed her.

Another group went hunting for the homeless to give them a goody bag. In a shopping centre they came across a man who had been homeless for seven days since his release from prison. They handed over a bag with essentials including bread, water and socks. The man was so grateful that somebody cared for him. He shared that his social worker was on holiday and the homeless shelters had closed for the weekend. Without this gift of love he would have been at a real loss.

Love is a guiding force in all we do; it is the password for much of the Christian walk. As this generation learn to love in a culture that is inherently selfish and full of hate, they will shine out in the darkness. This love is part of the DNA that God is building into the Josiah Generation so that they will be positioned to take care of the destitute and the hurting, to shepherd God's people just as King Josiah led the people of Israel.

One of our young leaders had a small group of nine children who she looked after each week. But she knew that this was not going to last forever. The next year she would be eleven and would be moving into secondary school. Worse still, she was going to a different school from all her friends.

Each time I spoke with her she had one overriding concern: "Who will look after my friends when I am not there to disciple them?" She was really burdened by this issue and prayed to God until she had a solution. Through the course of that year she raised up one of the group, who God had highlighted to her, to become the leader of the others. As a shepherd she could not simply abandon her sheep, but had to know that they would still be taken care of.

This is the heart of the Josiah Generation. Indeed, it is their love for God and their heart for people that will cause them to keep on going when they feel like giving up.

Sarah was on a mission with us and heard from God that she was going to meet an elderly lady called Margaret who had difficulty walking and multiple health problems. God wanted Margaret to know that He loved her.

When we arrived at the town it was full of elderly ladies using walking sticks. Sarah was undeterred and started to run around them all asking if their name was Margaret. Hours went by, but she had still not found her Margaret. She felt like giving up, but she just kept on going. Just as we were about to head home, Sarah saw an elderly lady with a stick that she had not yet spoken to. She ran up to her and offered her a cookie. "By any chance, is your name Margaret?"

When the lady replied "Yes" she was suddenly swamped by eight young people. She wondered what was happening to her as they explained that God had spoken to them about her. Sarah handed over the letter and as she read it she broke down in tears.

"How did you know? Tomorrow I am going into hospital because of my health problems."

Right there Sarah was able to pray for her. Miraculously, Margaret used to live just around the corner from our church, which was a couple of hours drive from the town we were in. God, through Sarah, had handpicked this lady for His purposes. Sarah could have given up, but she kept on going, knowing that because God had highlighted Margaret to her, she had a duty to fulfil.

As we have said, this Josiah Generation will be radical. Some will see that as a threat, others will regard them as mavericks. But there is more to them than a radical edge – they are also tender-hearted. Everything they are doing is because of their heart for God and their understanding of God's heart for people.

God's mercy

The Josiah Generation will have no mercy for structure, religion or tradition. If you want to get them fired up, let them know that they can't change the way things are, because that is how things have always been as long as can be remembered. Brought up in a fast changing, computer-driven world, keeping traditions for the sake of traditions will not be something that comes naturally to them. All this is part of God's shaping of a generation to fulfil His master plan.

They will however show God's mercy to people.

For those who serve in any ministry capacity within the church, it is easy for this to become the purpose of church for them. But God is more interested in us than He is in our ministry. He can do the things He is calling us to do through anyone, raising up whoever He chooses, whenever He chooses. But He wants to see us grow to become more like Jesus. That's why God can be ruthless with manmade organisations, allowing everything to crumble around us whilst still keeping us strong. He is more interested in who we are, than in what we do.

This focus on people, instead of structures, requires a relational version of church. It is countercultural to the world that this generation is growing up in, where young people can spend more time building virtual relationships through social networking sites than they spend investing in real friendships. Yet those in the Josiah Generation are called to be reformers, not simply within the church, but within their own generation.

One day we were driving to a church meeting when Joshua, my son, asked where we were going.

"We're going to church," I told him, with a smile.

"No, daddy, we are the church. What you mean is we are going to the building to meet with the church."

At that moment, my own words came back to slap me in the face. Here was my seven-year old son taking hold of his Josiah Generation anointing, ignoring the traditional ways of thinking and helping to correct me.

The revolution has begun. God's heart is being revealed through the next generation.

Are you ready?

12
A Driving Passion

"Now before him there was no king like him, who turned to the LORD
with all his heart, with all his soul, and with all his might, according to
all the Law of Moses; nor after him did any arise like him."

(2 Kings 23: 25)

Worship – a heart matter

Alicia was six years old and she was falling in love with God. When she
was at home, she would frequently go into her room just to worship
Him. Her worship came out of a simple, strong love for God. Each
day she would sing songs she knew and songs that she made up, at
the top of her voice. As the weeks went by you could see her life
radiating God more and more.

There was just one problem. Alicia's singing was so loud that the
neighbours were being disturbed.

Her parents had to sit with her and ask her to continue worshipping
God, but at a lower volume. Her heart was simply bursting with

worship for God so much that she could not help but sing loudly!

King Josiah's passion and zeal to live for God was something that showed in all he did. All his actions sought to restore worship to God. Worship was at the very heart of the move of God, for worshipping God is the very heart of our call as human beings. It's impossible to truly worship God without worship coming from the heart.

Alicia is not alone among the Josiah Generation in having a passion for worship. Many children and even babies love to worship God. I have known babies who rocked in their bouncers whenever songs of worship to God were sung, but interestingly did not respond in the same way to nursery rhymes or other music.

Simeon was aged four when he started having prolonged worship spells. Whenever he'd had a time of being especially close to God in a church meeting, he would come home and confine himself to his room. There he would make up his own songs to God, for over an hour, before coming back down. At the top of his voice he would pour out praise and worship from the intensity of his heart. No one told him to do it, no one even told him he could do it – he simply could not help but sing out in response to his encounters with God. Sometimes his brothers even teased him for his raucous singing, but this did not put him off, he just wanted to worship God with all his heart.

Passion for God – a driving force

In our contemporary world many people have lost all sense of purpose and with it a passion for life. Apathy sets in and with it, the sentiment that as long as I am okay, there is nothing that I need to do to bring about change. The generation referred to as Generation X has been typecast as those overcome with apathy and without a cause.

But a new generation is rising up after them. The generation nicknamed Generation Z by sociologists has also been known by some as the "dreamer generation", as they seek to dream of and bring about real change in the world. The Josiah Generation will not be a generation of apathy, but will show themselves as a generation of passion. This is not simply a passion for change for the sake of change, but a passion for God that requires change in each individual. That personal change will inspire change in those around them.

It is easy to be passionate about the wrong thing, whether it is the pursuit of wealth, the pursuit of popularity, or even the pursuit of peace. Such a passion drives people forward to overcome many obstacles. Indeed, anyone who is going to achieve anything of significance, in any field, will need to have a passion for their work. Without it, they will be quick to give up as obstacles are thrown across their path.

When we have a passion for something it invades every area of our lives. If you have a holiday that you are looking forward to, it will crop up in conversations with anyone you speak to, it will fill your spare time as you plan for it, and it will even invade your thought life while you are busy on another task.

Those whose passion is their work and the accumulation of wealth find their passion manifesting in their words, their actions and their thoughts. Passion crosses every part of our inner being.

However, a passion that is not focused on God will be unable to satisfy. Such a passion simply leads to a dead end, something the pursuant will eventually discover. A passion for wealth can be a strongly motivating factor, but the wealthy are not satisfied by their wealth. A passion for knowledge does not satisfy, and even those with a passion for close relationships will find themselves alone at times. But no matter what the passion that acts as the driving force in an individual's life, there will always be a desire for God bubbling under the surface.

This generation that God is raising up will be passionate both for Him and for His cause. This passion will be the driving force that will enable them to cut against the trends of society and the norms of their day to stand up for the kingdom of God.

The outsider looking on may wonder where the balance is in their life, but those with this passion just long for everyone else to be able to share it with them and to see things as they see them. Olympic athletes alter their whole lives, from sleeping patterns to diet, from training to rest, to focus on winning the prize. They will decline invitations to parties and allow their training to take centre stage, even over friendships and family commitments at times. An outsider may not understand what they are doing, but they will see the fruits of the training on the day of the race.

So the Josiah Generation will be driven to serve God with all their hearts. Outsiders may look at the sacrifices they are making and shy away from them, but for those with the passion for God, it does not even seem like a sacrifice at the time. Instead, it is just a simple act of obedience to God. In the final days, the fruit of their labours and sacrifice will be seen by all.

This passion enables them not only to hear God's call, but to act to fulfil it. King Josiah was clearly driven by this kind of divine passion, turning to God with all his heart, soul and strength. Every fibre of his being was devoted to fulfilling the call of God. His unstoppable quest for reform was driven by his immeasurable passion for God. In his life he lived up to the degree of revelation that he had received from God. As God revealed more of Himself and His plans, Josiah simply went along with them.

Josephine was nine years old when she joined a leadership training scheme. When she joined the course it was a simple act of obedience to God, even though she couldn't see herself as a leader. In fact, she felt a bit nervous about the idea of being a leader. One day she was praying to God when she heard God speak to her clearly. He told her that He was going to give her a small group in her school, with three people in it, for her to lead.

To some this word may not seem that significant. It does not have the dramatic sound of bringing revival to a school and seeing teachers swoon under the power of God. But to Josephine it was confirmation that God had called her to serve Him as a leader. She loved God so much that she simply had to act on what He had told her. With great courage she spoke to a few people and within a few months her passionate obedience to God's call saw the fulfilment of God's word. She was the leader of three people.

She had heard the call from God and simply obeyed. She demonstrated the tenacity that runs through the Josiah Generation when enacting all that God has equipped them to do. But Josephine's work did not stop there.

Having reached this target, God spoke to her again about the next step for her. God was calling her to grow the small group with the help of the first three people He had given to her, so that they could start to see change in their school. Again, characteristic of this generation, she started to pursue the fulfilment of this next stage of God's plan for her.

Infectious passion

To some passion is offensive.

The very nature of passion means that it can be seen even when someone is trying to hide it. It presents itself in a way that is visible, even when it is not seeking a platform. When someone is passionate about a subject, everyone who talks with them knows it. Unintentionally, it is in your face. Such a passion for God will offend some.

For others, passion is something that is misunderstood. They see an individual devoting much of their time to an area and don't really understand their motive or their motivation.

Instead of digging deeper to discover more, they heap judgment on the one who is passionate. In Christian circles this can happen in a more subtle manner:

"They may be passionate for God now, but it won't last..."

"They just need more balance in their life..."

When I was fourteen, my parents attended an open day at my

school. Whilst they were there, speaking with my various teachers, the Christian head teacher came over and asked to have a word with them.

"Your son," he reliably informed them, "is a bit over the top in his faith at the moment. He needs to calm down."

Looking back, I can see where he was coming from. He was keen to see me raised as a rounded individual and in my zeal as a youngster I did not always express everything in the right way. But his judgement of me demonstrated a lack of understanding as to what God was doing in me at that time.

After the open day was over my parents shared this conversation with me. They then told me how pleased they were with this report and encouraged me to keep on going for God with all my heart. Advice that I was only too pleased to follow!

Some of the children under our care have undergone real opposition. One child was threatened with exclusion for speaking about God; another started to receive obscene text messages from people when they began to speak about God. At these times, I have felt the weight of responsibility for their pastoral care. What would your reaction be if your children were being assaulted in these ways?

At times like this, some would seek to withdraw the children from the front line in an attempt to protect them. I have certainly gone back to God with a few questions myself. But in doing so, God invariably shows me that the children are not being tempted beyond what they can bear, but that they are being made stronger in Him. God always seems to bring them an answer in those difficult times. For me to stop them from serving God would be to misunderstand what God has called them to do. Instead, my role is to equip them with what they need so that they will be able to keep on standing as they face battles, not just as children, but throughout their adult lives.

Persecution is guaranteed for Christians. It is those who are grounded in God's Word who will be able to stand. So rather than sidestepping the issue or burying my head in the sand, as they grow in passion we are responsible for ensuring that this passion is truly rooted in the Word of God – not based on emotionalism or, worse still, manufactured by an environment created by man. A God-given passion is available to this Josiah Generation that will lead them on.

Whilst some will be offended and others will not understand this, there will be still others who will find the passion of the Josiah Generation infectious. As this generation is devoted in the extreme to God, this in itself will cause people to turn to Him. Just as a cold spreads around an office, some will take precautions to protect themselves while others will catch the bug.

Passion is infectious. I love watching the way that God takes an individual and sets them on fire for Him to the extent that those around them also start to experience change. One group of teenage boys started to egg each other on in their service to God. On Sundays they met and shared stories of the things God had done that week, then they went off to their separate schools, expectant that God would do even more.

Ore was a part of that group. He was as cool as a cucumber in everything that he did. He was one of those kids who was so cool that he didn't care what other people thought of him. He was simply willing to be himself. At the same time, he was so streetwise that I was concerned about what might happen to him. It seemed he was heading towards the wrong group and gradually picking up their habits.

When a couple of the members of his Sunday group started to get passionate for God, Ore went with the flow. He had already experienced God for himself and this was just the encouragement he needed to live it out. Before long he had led several of his friends to Jesus and was meeting with them regularly to help them know Him more. He still remained uniquely cool, but now had a godly glow about him that was drawing his friends into the church.

The infectious passion of the friends he met on Sundays was now part of his life and was spreading to his friends in school. Ore, in his own laid back style, was serving God with all of his heart.

The Josiah Generation will serve God with every fibre of their being. Their fire will burn strong. Such passion demands a response. The response may be positive or negative, but in the face of such raw passion it cannot be neutral. When you get close to the fire, you either try to put out the fire, move away because you can't stand the heat, or you get set alight yourself. In the same way the passion of the Josiah Generation will either see people oppose them, distance themselves, or allow a flame to be ignited inside them.

13
Since the Time
of the Judges

*"There had been no Passover kept in Israel like that since the days of
Samuel the prophet; and none of the kings of Israel had kept such a
Passover as Josiah kept, with the priests and the Levites, all Judah and
Israel who were present, and the inhabitants of Jerusalem."*
(2 Chronicles 35:18)

Waiting for the season
of the grape

One day when we were praying, my wife had a prophetic word: "The
season of the apple is over, the season of the banana is now here, but
the season of the grape is still to come." Those who heard it thought
she had turned into a fruit case – until she explained it. This word was
all to do with the way the harvest is gathered in.

When we pick apples we take them off the tree one at a time.
Up until this point, this is what we had seen God doing through the
children as they led their friends to the Lord one at a time. When

you harvest bananas you pick them in bunches, perhaps in tens. But, when you harvest grapes, you pick them in their hundreds.

From the day this word was given we started to hear testimonies from the children about how they had led several of their friends to the Lord, all on the same day. God seemed to be giving them the harvest in bunches, just like you pick bananas.

Then one day, God allowed us to hear a testimony that whetted our appetite for the "season of the grape".

Jordan was a confident thirteen-year old who loved God and loved talking about Him. One day in school he decided it had been too long since he had told anyone about God. That morning, after registration, while his class was sitting around chatting and waiting for the first lesson to start, he spoke to the teacher who was supervising them.

"Sir, is it okay if I speak to all the boys in the class."

The teacher gave his consent and they all gathered around Jordan.

"Right, put your hands up if you believe in God," Jordan started, lifting his own hand in the air. A quick scan of the room showed that his was to be the only hand going up that day. Jordan started to tell them why he believed in God and encouraged them to think about Him and even to follow Him. The teacher interrupted Jordan and told him to stop talking such nonsense.

Stopped in mid flow, Jordan invited anyone who wanted to hear more to meet him in the middle of the school playing field during break time.

That break time Jordan went to the playing field hoping that a couple of people from his class would come to hear more. But when he got to the field he was in for a real surprise. There, waiting for him, were around ninety children from various classes who had heard of the conversation he'd started earlier but had been made to stop. There and then, Jordan got to share the gospel with ninety people who wanted to know more.

Several people joined his group and though the harvest was not in its hundreds, it was a taste of what God could do when He chooses to.

This Josiah Generation are called to do extraordinary exploits for God beyond anything that has been seen for generations in our nations.

King Josiah himself was the instigator of such a move. As he served God faithfully and devoutly, he brought real change to the spiritual landscape around him. In destroying the idols, removing the false priests and roaming across the whole nation of Israel, we have seen that Josiah brought real change to the nation. But nowhere is the extent of his actions spelt out more clearly than in the description of the Passover he celebrated. This Passover was of the kind that people had not seen for generations, though some had dreamt of it and longed for it.

Imagine if God were to raise up thousands of people, each of whom were given the kind of opportunities that Jordan had that day. Imagine if we were living in the season of the grape, with hundreds coming to know the Lord at a time. This is what many people have been longing for over many years. But imagine if it started to happen with this generation.

When King Josiah held his Passover, all the people around him were ready and prepared for the celebration. Not only did Josiah lead the way in giving sacrifices, but all the officials gave from their own resources to make sure this was a special occasion. When you read the account in Scripture, you get the impression that the writer can't put into words the experience, so instead he gives us this curious phrase: *"There had been no Passover kept in Israel like that since the days of Samuel the prophet; and **none** of the kings of Israel had kept such a Passover as Josiah kept."* (2 Chronicles 35:18)

On the face of it, these words may seem like an exaggerated account, but when we look at the account of a similar celebration given a few chapters earlier, you can see that the writer is actually trying to give an accurate account of what took place. King Hezekiah had held an incredible Passover feast not so long ago. Hezekiah was king before Josiah's grandfather, Manasseh. Memory of his actions would still be spoken about; the older members of society would already have compared Josiah to his great grandfather, Hezekiah, and recalled all he had done. These stories of reform would no doubt have been circulating even among the younger generation.

The description of King Hezekiah's celebration is simply exquisite. It seems like the greatest celebration that you can imagine. In fact, the way it is written, it contains echoes of another great celebration that has been recorded, the opening of the temple under King Solomon. In 2 Chronicles 30:26 Hezekiah's Passover is compared all the way back to the time of Solomon and David. It was such an experience that, when the Passover week was over, everybody decided to keep on celebrating for another week.

When that second week was over, the people went out into the streets and tore down the false idols and altars. Their hearts had been touched so deeply that they desired change. Hezekiah's Passover was remarkable, not only as an experience for those who were there, but also as a point of change.

But, when it comes to Josiah's celebration, the writer limits his words as he tries to describe it. He simply says it was greater than any that had gone before. It was greater than the rose tinted memories people had of Hezekiah's Passover. And more remarkable still, it was greater than those held by the kings of the United Kingdom of Israel. King Solomon who built the temple and King David who had a heart after God both held grand celebrations, but King Josiah's topped the bill.

The judges followed directly on from Moses' time, when the Passover was first celebrated. Those early celebrations must have been significant, as some of the children from the first Passover, who went on to possess the Promised Land, gathered with their children and shared the stories. Thousands of years later it is not hard for us to imagine the atmosphere there must have been as each year they recalled their deliverance, first from Egypt and then from the desert wanderings, remembering that now not only were they no longer slaves, but they were also living in a land of milk and honey. Their

Passovers must have been poignant moments in the annual calendar, reminding them of their recent history. And King Josiah's Passover is compared to that.

Josiah could not have done anything further to improve this celebration in honour of God. This is a gold standard fulfilment of God's call, living it out to the full. This is the destiny of the Josiah Generation.

A dollop of God

Children's pastors all want to run successful children's programmes and see them flourish in the fullest way possible. Around the world there are many different ways that they try to achieve this.

For some, the answer is to throw lots of money at the ministry. Don't get me wrong, money is very useful. I would love to oversee a ministry to children that had an unlimited budget and full access to every resource imaginable. The spending of money on the next generation of church makes a statement on behalf of the church leadership that demonstrates the value they place on the ministry. But even with the best building in the world, the most gifted staff, the most professional looking props, and the highest value placed on the ministry by the leadership, this does not mean that the children will get close to God.

Others react against the "church is boring" sentiment and seek to make church the most exciting place to be. Competing with the world's standards of entertainment, with games at the very centre of each programme, they plan to keep the children coming back week after week. A regular sprinkling of sweets adds to the notion that church is the highlight of the week and for the children it may well be. I personally love playing games with children and seeing the delight on their faces, but just because children are enjoying themselves does not mean that they are getting closer to God.

Others seek to keep the children coming by getting them involved.

If each child has a job or a responsibility, or even a part in a play, then they are more likely to come back next week. This is certainly true, but it does not mean that the children will get close to God. Indeed, we may even be doing them a disservice by allowing them to serve God before they have really encountered Him for themselves. After all, our service is a response to our love for Him, not the basis of it.

There are adults who are confused about this matter, feeling that they have to do something in the church to be accepted by God, instead of doing something in the church *because* they are accepted by Him. I believe we need to tread very carefully if we are going to get children involved in ministry roles before they have really encountered God for themselves.

For others, the ministry is all about the relationships they build with the children. They roll up their sleeves and ensure that the children know they are loved. I do not deny that this is a very important factor. When they encounter a leader, the children should experience the love of God through that leader. But if this is all we do, then we have become a volunteer division of social services, meeting the children's emotional needs.

In many places I have been to, the Bible is offered after one of these sweeteners, smuggled in almost apologetically as the bit we do because we are "at church" before we get on to the bit that we came for. Underlying this approach is the fear that if we focus primarily on the spiritual part, the children won't be interested. But when Jesus came to earth He was the star attraction. If Jesus was here, I am sure that He would play games, love the children, share sweets with them and want them to have the best resources that money could buy. But more than that, Jesus would want them to have HIM. The children would enjoy all those other things, but Jesus would be the reason that they hung around.

Of course, the above descriptions are typecasts. I guess we are all in danger of slipping into one of them to some degree at different times. The real answer is to keep our focus on the key thing.

The children need to encounter God for themselves.

If a big dollop of God lands on them, they will not be the same. God does not need any gimmicks to hold the children; He just needs space to move. Some people are nervous, thinking, albeit subconsciously, that God will not be able to hold the children's attention. But when He turns up, the real problem is not getting them to stay, but getting them to leave.

The only time I can remember a young person feeling uncomfortable in a meeting where God showed up was when one particular young man came to visit us for the first time. Talking to him afterwards he was clearly freaked out. He told me plainly why: "I am an Emo and a Satanist. These people are all my age and every single one of them was smiling. It's obvious they weren't on drugs, they were just so happy. I couldn't stand it in there."

In Josiah's time, after all the different fads that the nation had been through, God suddenly became fashionable again. Through all of Josiah's work, God was the star attraction when the people met together. What an exciting time it must have been to live in, when even those who did not believe were forced to consider God because of the environment they were in.

As our programmes, meetings and indeed lives become overtly God-focused, the next generation will be drawn in. When we cultivate an environment where God is at the centre, He then has the space to do something special. It is easy for our energy and time to be drawn into practical details with the spiritual side being left until last, but this is the most important aspect of the ministry. When we give our time in prayer, then God meets with the children and they grow closer to Him.

On one occasion we gathered together a number of young teens and encouraged them to invite their friends as we met with God. We began the time with worship and many of the young people just opened up their hearts to God in worship and lifted their hands to Him.

In the middle of the room I spotted a visitor. It was her first time at a church meeting and looking around the room, she found it understandably funny to see these teenagers worshipping God in this way. She smiled and looked over to her friend who had invited her to share the joke, only to discover that her friend was also worshipping God in the same way. Not wanting to be out of place, the visitor closed her eyes and half lifted her hands.

Because of the environment, she moved from a place of watching others to opening her heart up to God. She met with God at that moment and was never going to be the same again. By the time we had shared God's Word, she was ready to respond to the gospel and in the years that followed she went on to flourish in her walk with God.

As we make God the focus of our programmes for this generation, we are preparing them for the supernatural things that He has planned for them. This preparation is vital if this generation is to be used by God in ways that, until now, we have only dreamed of.

A move that has been prepared

When Hezekiah held his Passover the people were not really prepared for the move of God. It was an awesome time, but as we have seen, compared to the Passover held under Josiah there was still room for improvement.

In the time of King Hezekiah, not enough priests had consecrated themselves to cope with the move of God – they had failed to prepare themselves. Also, the land itself was still full of idols, implying that many of the Israelites were divided in their worship between the idols and the living God when the Passover was reinstated. By the time Josiah got round to holding the Passover, all these issues had been sorted out. The foundation had been laid for a significant move of God.

In my early days of ministering to children, I went to a church where God had recently been using the children in a very powerful way. The children had been praying for the adults in the main service and incredible miracles had been taking place. Several months on from that event, people were still buzzing about how much God had used the children.

When they shared these stories with me, I was immediately interested and wanted to find out more. "What preparation had the children been given for this move of God?" I asked. My question was greeted with blank faces. "Well, what took place after God had used the children? How did the leaders follow it up?" I wanted to know. There were more blank looks and a few mumbles of "nothing really happened."

I left that place feeling sad. We can't control a move of God, but we can prepare for it. It seemed that this church had failed not only to prepare for it, but also to follow up after it and consolidate all that had taken place in the lives of the children.

King Josiah had clearly prepared the people through all his hard work for the Passover and when the time came they were ready to respond. We have a responsibility to this generation, to ensure that they are fully prepared for the work that God has called them to. We may not fully know the details of how God will use them, that is His business, but we do know that He has great plans for this emerging generation.

14

Leaving
A Legacy

"Thus Josiah removed all the abominations from all the country that belonged to the children of Israel, and made all who were present in Israel diligently serve the LORD their God. All his days they did not depart from following the LORD God of their fathers."

(2 Chronicles 34:33)

The life of Josiah

Once Josiah had finished his reforms, he carried on living for God. Having cleaned up the country, he kept it clean. The people followed God for all of Josiah's life. The Josiah Generation will have this same influence on those around them. Their influence is not an overnight wonder, but a statement of real change. As they grow older, the battles they once fought will remain victories for the kingdom as long as they live.

It is such a delight to see those in whom we have invested growing up to live for God as they pass through their teenage years and on into adulthood. Recently a lady came and asked to speak with me. I presumed her to be a parent and took her to one side. She shared how, at the age of twelve, she had met with God in such a profound way as she had attended the children's ministry. Now, over ten years later she has been serving God faithfully all that time. I did not recognise her face, though her name was familiar, but she knew her life had been set on a completely new course by her early encounters with God.

The lives of the Josiah Generation will be marked by a continual pursuit of God after that first meeting with Him, influencing those around them and keeping Him central in every part of their lives. Throughout this book we have outlined the potential stored in this generation whilst they are alive, but the question still remains, what will their long term legacy be?

The death of Josiah

Josiah's death brings a timely warning for the Josiah Generation. Josiah was a man of zeal. He attacked every task with boundless energy and unstoppable enthusiasm. So, when he heard that there was a war to fight Josiah was ready to lead his army into it.

The King of Egypt had gone to fight in a place called Carchemish, hundreds of miles away from any land that Israel had ever occupied. They had to pass through the land of Israel to get there and, even though they did not go through the kingdom of Judah, Josiah was still ready to fight.

At this point the King of Egypt did not want to fight against the kingdom of Judah. His target was not even the wider kingdom of Israel. He was simply passing through on his way to an old adversary. This was not Josiah's battle and the Egyptians were not his enemy. Though King Josiah may have perceived them as a threat, they were actually heading off to fight against the Babylonians, who would soon lead the kingdom of Judah into exile.

The king of Egypt sent a note of warning to Josiah, telling him that he was moving on God's orders. The king of Egypt reported everything that God had told him to do and instructed Josiah to keep out of it or risk opposing God's plans. But Josiah did not heed the warning, though it was genuinely from God.

Here, right at the end of his life, Josiah suffers an untimely end. Perhaps his own stubbornness or confidence in his previous exploits, or perhaps an arrogance that God would only speak to him directly, led him to fight against the Egyptians. Whatever the reason for his decision, it seems out of step for a man who the whole of his life was careful to obey God in the smallest detail. At the cost of his life, Josiah discovered that it had been God speaking to the king of Egypt after all. Early in the battle he was shot by an arrow and later died at the age of thirty-nine.

Having lived most of his life fighting the right battle at the right time, Josiah died fighting the wrong battle at the wrong time. Josiah's call had been to the geographical area of Israel, but in his death he stepped outside the remit of this call. Through his life he had had prophets around him, who had encouraged him in his labour for the Lord, but now, right at the end of his life, he was derailed. None of this detracted from the work he had done, but it was an abrupt ending to his calling.

The same zeal that had brought so much life to the kingdom ended up leading him to his death.

All humans are fallible and not one of us can claim to have received a completely pure revelation from God. That's why God has given us the Scriptures to search through and learn from. Somehow, through the mess of our lives, God always accomplishes His task. He is not dependent on any individual or even a generation. Each one of us is expendable, yet God chooses to call us and use us to further His plans. As the Josiah Generation are used by God they will need to keep such a humble perspective to avoid ending up spiritually shipwrecked.

I believe that, in this, we have a real warning for the Josiah

Generation. Many of them will do great things for God, but at the same time they will still require the older generation to be there for them, even after they have done great exploits. If we are careful not to oppose them when they are serving God in a radical form, but instead encourage them in their call, then we will have the right to speak into their lives if they deviate from God's plans. This will require much discernment – to know when to keep quiet and allow them to teach us things about God, and when to speak up and influence them.

This warning may be solemn, but it gives us an additional point of focus as we prepare this generation for their call. As we train them from a young age, there is a responsibility on us as parents and leaders to help them know how to hear from God and how to study His Word. If they can learn to live humbly before God, appreciating the generations of church that have gone before them, all this will help them to be open to the guidance of other people, especially if those same people have proved supportive of them when they have got it right.

One young man who I worked with was being drawn away from God by a love for football. We had an open chat about it and he made the difficult decision to put God first, no matter what the cost. Later on he was able to look back and see that he had made the right decision. In rejecting something that had become an idol to him, he accepted his call from God. As the anointing God had put on him became more evident within the church and people tried to pull him in many directions, he was always open to any guidance I had to offer, because of the way I had helped him make the right decision concerning his relationship with God. With such a responsibility given to me, I was very careful to encourage him lots and advise him little – other than at times when his love for God was cooling.

For this generation, the right to speak into their lives in this way is not a given, especially as they will be fighting against some of the traditions that we have gone along with in our own lives. The right is earned as we support them, recognising the call of God on their lives. As Paul puts it, you have many teachers, but you do not have many fathers. We have a responsibility to father this generation, giving them the freedom to serve God whilst always being available to guide them when required.

The legacy of Josiah

Within three months of Josiah's death the kingdom of Judah was invaded by the Egyptians, a new king was appointed, and the nation had to pay great sums of money to Egypt. A decade later things went from bad to worse as the king of Babylon turned up and took over the nation, leading some of its inhabitants into exile.

On the face of it, it looks like Josiah's lifetime work had been overturned in an instant. In our current times there is that same danger of the work of God seemingly being undone in a moment.

There are many prophecies that speak of increasing persecution coming to Christians in the Western world. The Bible tells us that evil will continue up to the end of time and that the kingdom of darkness will grow stronger alongside the kingdom of God.

It may be that in these last days some will question the impact of this generation. But whatever follows on from their work, it is clear that none of their service will be wasted. Indeed, I would go so far as to say that they are essential to paving the way for the days ahead – especially if those days are to contain much darkness.

Josiah's reforms were actually needed for the Israelites to be able to survive in exile.

Firstly, through Josiah's reforms, people could understand what God was doing. The teachings of the Law made it clear that the nation was being punished for its former sins. God was still in the picture.

When we see current events through the framework of Scripture, we can always see God at work in the world.

Even if we don't understand His precise methodology, we know He is still working towards the same master plan for the world.

Secondly, Josiah's legacy was not simply in the revival of the teachings, but in the deposit that was left in individual's lives. The impact Josiah's reign had in the long term could not be fully recorded because of the number of people's lives that were influenced by it. But we do see mention of some very significant ministries which were either birthed or developed under Josiah's rule.

Jeremiah, one of the greatest prophets of the Old Testament era, began prophesying in the thirteenth year of Josiah's reign. This took place soon after Josiah had begun to purge the nation of idols, but before the building of the temple. The prophetic call on Jeremiah's life continued as the people were taken into exile by the Babylonians and his prophetic words still carry meaning for us today.

Two minor prophets, Zephaniah and Habakkuk, also ran their prophetic ministry during the time of Josiah.

But Josiah's legacy goes beyond those who were prophesying when he was alive. When the Babylonians dragged some of the Israelites around eleven years after Josiah's death, four young men were among those who were taken away. Daniel, Shadrach, Meshach and Abednego all had a substantial influence in their adopted home because they refused to yield to the pressure to worship its foreign gods. Daniel's long life serving as a ruler in the most powerful nation of his time, advising several generations of kings and receiving dreams concerning the end times, marked him out even from the other three.

Such a strong foundation of God must have stemmed from their childhoods for they had barely reached adulthood when they were taken from their homeland.

As children, they would have lived in a nation where the idols were still kept at bay and the worship of God took centre stage. Through their childhood they would not have known any other gods, because the king had seen to it that they were all removed years earlier.

And so the continuation of the kingdom of God was passed on to the next generation. Josiah may have failed to influence his children directly, as each of them failed to live up to the standards he had set. Perhaps Josiah was too caught up in running the country and ministering to the Lord. But he certainly succeeded in creating an environment where the whole of the next generation could be influenced to also walk with the Lord.

This desire to pass on what they have received to the next generation is something that I have seen in a few of the Josiah Generation. They want to see the younger children have the same experiences with God that they have had. They value their spiritual foundation and want to pass it on to the next generation. The children love to see those close to their age encouraging them in their faith and sharing their experiences of God, and the young people who desire to do this gain great satisfaction from it. After all, disicipling those around is a primary mandate that God has given to each one of us.

As we focus on passing on our faith to the generation who follow us, may they rise up and not only fulfil their call, but also prepare those who will come after them to hand on the baton of faith in an ever purer form – until the bride of Christ is prepared and Jesus returns.

The Josiah Generation is rising up, the bride is being prepared.
Amen. Come, Lord Jesus.

Questions for Personal Reflection or Group Discussion

1. Think about your ministry to the youngest children of your family and the church:

> a. In what ways are you ministering to them and preparing them for their future call?
>
> b. What more can you do to prepare them for their future?

2. Think about your ministry to the older children of your family and the church:

> a. What opportunities do these children have to serve God?
>
> b. How effective are you at equipping them to serve God in their schools?
>
> c. What support do you have in place for them as they serve God?
>
> d. What more can you do to prepare and release them into their call?

3. Think about the changes the Josiah generation may bring to the church:

> a. Are you ready to give the next generation the freedom to change structures?
>
> b. What things do you think may be changed where you are?

4. Think about the support you can offer this generation as they grow up:

> a. Are you ready to encourage them in their call as they bring about reformation (in spite of any personal discomfort this may cause)?
>
> b. How will you ensure you are in a position of trust with this generation, so that they will listen to you if they stray in any way from the Bible's framework?

Read it Yourself

Read the entire story of King Josiah in 2 Kings chapters 22-23 and 2 Chronicles chapters 34-35.

About the
Author

Olly Goldenberg has been ministering to children, both in churches and outside of the church, for over twenty years. For fifteen of those years he was the children's pastor at Kensington Temple, serving one of the largest children's ministries in Europe.

Recently Olly founded the ministry *Children Can* and travels around inspiring churches and equipping leaders that their children and young people can do all things through Christ. He currently lives in London with his wife and four sons.

Notes